YEAR *of* PLENTY

One Suburban Family, Four Rules, and 365 Days of
Homegrown Adventure in Pursuit of Christian Living

CRAIG L. GOODWIN

All the best
on your journey of Plenty.

To Noel and Lily

YEAR OF PLENTY
One Suburban Family, Four Rules, and 365 Days of Homegrown Adventure in Pursuit of Christian Living

All biblical citations are taken from Today's New International Version unless otherwise noted. (Grand Rapids, Mich.: Zondervan, 2005).

Cover design: Alisha Lofgren
Book design: Michelle Cook/4 Seasons Book Design

Library of Congress Cataloging-in-Publication Data

Goodwin, Craig (Craig L.)
Year of plenty : one suburban family, four rules, and 365 days of homegrown adventure in pursuit of Christian living / Craig Goodwin.
  p. cm.
Includes bibliographical references and index.
ISBN 978-1-4514-0074-8 (alk. paper)
1. Goodwin family. 2. Goodwin, Craig (Craig L.) 3. Christian biography. 4. Christian life. I. Title.
BR1702.G8 2011
277.3'0830922--dc22
[B]
                                    2011003710

Manufactured in the U.S.A.

15   14   13   12   3   4   5   6   7   8   9   10

Contents

Acknowledgments

MY HEART IS FULL WITH GRATITUDE AS I REFLECT ON THE process of writing this book. At the center of this thankfulness is my family. I am blessed beyond measure by my daughters, Noel and Lily. Their creativity, laughter, and tenderness are an inspiration. My remarkable wife, Nancy, has been an ever-present source of unconditional grace and encouragement. I want to thank her for the ways that she has nourished our family with the key ingredients of joy, love, and forgiveness. She has been unreasonably patient as I've transformed our quaint suburban residence into a small farm. It is a privilege to stand with her as a pastoral colleague and fellow adventurer in the way of Jesus.

This book is, in part, a reflection on my pilgrimage of coming to faith in Christ and following a call to ministry in the Presbyterian Church. As I look back on that journey, I am especially thankful for Steve Bodwell's passionate faith, for Denny Rydberg's winsome spirit, and for Earl Palmer's earthy intellect. I feel fortunate to have been shaped by the wonderful diversity of Fuller Theological Seminary, and I want to thank Alan Roxburgh and Mark Lau Branson for luring me down the missional rabbit hole into a generative conversation about leadership in today's church.

Our story is also a reflection of the church communities that have shaped us through the years. These include Maple Valley Presbyterian near Seattle, Bel Air Presbyterian in Los Angeles, University Presbyterian in Seattle, Clear Lake Presbyterian in Houston, and Millwood Presbyterian Church here in Spokane. There is so much talk about the decline of mainline denominations as if God is not at work within their bounds, but that certainly hasn't been our experience. Every one of these churches has been a vital expression of God's Spirit alive in our midst and leading us to Jesus at every turn.

There are distant voices that have been close companions in the shaping of our year-long experiment. These include the writings of Barbara Kingsolver, Eugene Peterson, Michael Pollan, and Wendell Berry. The fellow travelers at the *Year of Plenty* blog have also offered important input. Karen Dunlap and Keith Vetter have been particularly faithful conversation partners. Brad Thiessen and Doug Satre have also been good friends along the journey.

I am grateful for the farmers and artisans from the Millwood Farmers' Market who have mentored me in my agricultural pursuits and spurred me to consider the bigger picture of what God is doing in the world. Tom and Louise Tuffin, Gary and So Angell, Dave McCullough, and Antonio Macias have been especially helpful as partners in this work.

Our story was facilitated, in part, by our wonderful neighbors, Mark and Kristen Nicholson and their children Jacob and Jenna. Instead of reporting the growth of our suburban farm to county officials, they joined us as coconspirators—raising chickens, planting gardens, and helping establish a neighborhood black market of peanut butter and chocolate.

As a first-time author, I have been well-served by a small army of people. Thanks to Tony Jones and Tim Paulson for believing I had a book in me long before such belief was warranted. Thanks to Will Bergkamp, Joshua Messner, and Andrew DeYoung at sparkhouse and Augsburg Fortress for shepherding me through the publishing process and to Alisha Lofgren for the cover design that so beautifully captures the story of the book. I can't offer enough praise for Carla Barnhill and her skills editing the manuscript and pointing me in the right direction when I got lost in the tall grass.

Special thanks to Dan Hansen and Tana Young for their insights on the first draft and to Doug Sadler and Josh Terry for taking on the task of putting together a small-group curriculum to go with the book.

Finally, I'd like to thank my father and mother, Craig and Judy, and my sister Hillary, for the questions and answers they have shaped in me through the years. The fingerprints of that formation are all over the pages of this book.

Foreword

THIS ENGAGING BOOK GOT ITS START IN AN IMPROBABLE setting. Two Presbyterian pastors, man and wife, were in a restaurant having an evening meal of Pad Thai. It was two days after Christmas in 2007. They were unhappily recovering from a severe holiday hangover induced by a month of consumer binging on Christmas presents, a consumer wasteland. On the spot, they decided they didn't want to live this way any longer and set 2008 as a year of intentional living. They had three days to prepare themselves. This is the story of that year. It is a story honestly and modestly told—no apocalytptic ranting, no preaching, no pontificating. And very much a *story*—the detailed account, with insight and humor, of a suburban family with two pre-teenage daughters negotiating a way of life through the maze of American consumerism.

Albert Borgmann writes convincingly of the necessity, if we are not going to be ruined by living in a consumerist culture, of developing what he calls "focal practices"—practices that keep our lives attentive and present and participating in what is immediate and personal. Craig and Nancy Goodwin with their daughters are providing the rest of us with an unpretentious witness to just what is involved in focal practices.

The embracing context for this story as it is told here is the Word that became flesh, moved into our neighborhood—think of it, our very backyards!—and revealed God to us. Care of creation (environmentalism) is fundamentally about this incarnation, the core doctrine of the Christian faith, God with us in the Jesus of history.

But this is hard to take in. *Year of Plenty* goes a long way to help us take it in. We keep wanting to spiritualize Jesus, but our four gospel writers vehemently insist that Jesus was human, *very* human, the same kind of human as you, as me. He walked the paths and roads in first century Palestine just as I walk on sidewalks and trails in twenty-first century America. Jesus spent nine months in the womb just as I did. He was born of a woman just as I was. There was a family. There are named friends. There was work to do, carpentry and masonry and fishing. Meals were eaten. Prayers were prayed. He went in and out of houses and synagogues and the temple, just as we do in houses and schools and Walmarts and churches. He died and was buried, just as we will and will be.

This takes a great deal of the guesswork out of knowing God. Do you want to know what God is like, the form in which God reveals himself? Look in the mirror, look at your friends, look at your spouse. Start here: a human being with eyes and ears, hands and feet, an appetite and curiosity, eating meals with family and friends, walking to the store for a bottle of milk, hiking in the hills picking wildflowers, catching fish and cooking them on a beach for breakfast with your children.

Four writers were assigned by God's Holy Spirit the task of writing down the story of this God-with-us Jesus who lived in first century Palestine. They all write essentially the same story but with variations. But the one thing that they are totally agreed upon is that this Jesus, this God-revealing Jesus, was an actual, human person who lived his life in the identical conditions in which we live ours. No special effects, no dazzling angelic interventions, no levitations. Simple and thoroughly feet-on-the-ground ordinary. There was a brief moment one night in a boat caught in a storm on Lake Galilee, it lasted maybe ten seconds at the most, when his friends thought he was a ghost, but they quickly realized that they were wrong. There was a later occasion three days after they had watched him die on a cross when they again thought Jesus was a ghost.

Wrong again. There was no question. Jesus was totally human, just like them.

In another New Testament piece of writing, the Letter to the Hebrews, this thoroughly human Jesus is affirmed but with one exception: he was "without sin." Otherwise he lived and experienced it all, everything that goes into the human condition—weakness, limitations, temptations, suffering, celebration, outrage, hunger, thirst, sorrow, birth, death—the works.

What this means, and it is the task of the Christian community to insist on this, is that Jesus is not a principle or an idea or a truth—nothing abstract, nothing in general, nothing impersonal, nothing grandiose. When God revealed himself definitively he did it in a human body, an incarnation.

There is, of course, more to it than this. Jesus is not *just* human; he is also divine. Not only very human but very God. But what we have to face first of all, and what the Gospel writers do face, is that the divinity does not diminish so much as by a fingernail, doesn't dilute even by as much as a teardrop, the humanity. There is this holy mystery: Jesus at the same time that he is fully human with and for us is also God fully present to us, breathing the very Holy Spirit of God into us, enacting salvation and eternal life in us. But first of all—our four Gospel writers are emphatic in their witness—we are told in no uncertain terms that God became flesh, the human flesh of Jesus, and lived among us. We start with the human. This is the way God makes himself known to us.

One would think that this would be enthusiastically embraced as good news—unqualified good news. The surprise is that it is not. When it comes right down to it, I would rather become godlike than that God become like me. It turns out that a lot of us, more times than we like to admit it, aren't all that excited that a very human Jesus is revealing God to us. We have our own ideas of what we want God to be like. We keep looking around for a style of so-called spirituality that gives some promise that we can be godlike, be in control of our lives and the lives of others, exercise godlike authority or at least be authorities on God. Contemporary technology and the consumerism that develops out of it seem to promise something godlike.

When the know-it-all serpent promised our first parents that they could be "like God" we can be sure that they were not thinking of anything as ordinary as being human with all the limitations of being human. They were thinking of something far grander—knowing everything there is to know and getting an edge on the rest of the creation. When they heard those words from the serpent, "like God," we can easily imagine what went on in their heads: power, control, being in charge of everything, knowing everything, getting their own way, indulging every whim, able to do anything they desired without restriction.

The usual way we try to become like God is to first eliminate the God who reveals himself in human form and re-imagine God as the god I want to be, then invest this re-imagined god with our own god-fantasies and take charge of the god-business.

The old term for this re-imagined, replacement god is idolatry. It is without question the most popular religion in town—any town—and it always has been. In previous generations these idolatry gods were made of wood and stone, of gold and silver. The replacement god most in evidence in our generation is consumerism.

Year of Plenty is a gentle but insistent exposé of this consumerist replacement god. It is also a convincing witness to the sanctity of the everyday, the ordinary, the things we eat and clothes we wear, the names of our neighbors and the money we spend, which is to say, Jesus in our neighborhood.

Eugene H. Peterson
Professor Emeritus of Spiritual Theology
Regent College, Vancouver B.C.

CHAPTER 1

The Winter *of* Our Discontent

OUR STORY BEGINS ON DECEMBER 27, 2007, IN THE WAKE of a post-Christmas funk. This season of hyperconsumption somehow managed to leave us flat, disconnected from the stuff we were buying, and no better connected to family and friends than we'd been a month before. Instead of a thoughtful exchange of gracious gifts, Christmas felt more like a warm-hearted system of payoffs and buyouts.

Still staggering from our holiday hangover, my wife, Nancy, and I had a night on the town without our daughters, Noel, who was 7 at the time, and Lily, who was 5. Of all things, we went shopping. We were on our way out of a big-box bookstore when large, red clearance signs beckoned us like a porch light beckons moths. We needed a birthday present for a niece and decided on a sardine-can-sized manicure set housed in two square feet of cardboard and plastic. It was our last great deal of the season.

As we drove around in the cold, wet darkness of Seattle looking for a restaurant, there was an uneasy silence between us. Maybe it was the breakdown of our car earlier in the evening or the typical emotional overload of two pastors having just completed the

Christmas gauntlet of worship services, but I couldn't fight the creeping frustration that had been building in me for weeks. I glanced over at our latest acquisition and thought to myself, *That really is a piece of crap.* Normally I would be content to keep such thoughts to myself, but for some reason I felt led to proclaim it to the world. And I did.

"What do you mean? You were the one who said we should buy it," Nancy replied.

She had me there. I was the one who insisted we just get it and get out of there. Buying is like that for me sometimes. I just want to get it over with so I can put an end to the deafening dialogue in my head—the detailed cost-benefit analysis, the effort to focus on one thing in the midst of thousands, the urgency of detecting an apparent seam of weakness in the marketplace, the nagging recognition that whatever I purchase will soon join the scrap heap of useless consumer trash.

At this point I pulled the car off the road and into a parking lot, where I commenced to pour out my discontent. "Almost all of our recent purchases have been meaningless," I said. I lamented that they were far short of expressions of love. They were expensive. They were unnecessary accessories in the lives of relatively wealthy people. They preoccupied us for the better part of a month, bringing tension and anxiety to the busiest season of our work life.

Nancy listened to my little tirade and then responded, saying, "I'm sorry you feel that way, but I'm the one who has carried the majority of the burden of entertaining and gift buying and family communications. The weight of all of it has stressed me out and pushed me to the limit. If anyone has a right to complain about things, it's me."

So there we sat, in an empty strip mall parking lot, in a stalemate of discontent, wondering how such a festive season had led us to such a desolate place.

We moved our conversation to a Thai restaurant. Between sips of Tom Yon Goong soup, we tried to get some perspective on where we had gone wrong. We talked about the last-minute presents I purchased for the girls out of a fear that they might not have enough, only to see both of them surrounded by a small mountain of gifts on Christmas morning. How could we have ever worried about them running low on stuffed animals and video games? We reflected on how intentional our expressions of faith had been during Advent with worship and study, but how there seemed to be no meaningful connection between the rhythms of faith and our life of consumption. Not only that, we didn't seem to have much of a grasp on what was driving our consumer lives. Our Christmas lament quickly turned into a more general inquiry into the state of our family economy. We recognized that the fear of not having enough and the compulsion to buy more stuff were year-long companions. We were shoppers all year, but during the holidays we were shoppers on steroids. We were insatiable seekers, hungry for more, bottomless pits of want.

At some point in the conversation Nancy asked, "What could we do differently?" It was such a simple question but a simple answer was beyond our immediate reach. It was like asking a fish to consider alternatives to a water habitat. We had been swimming in mindless consumerism for so long it was hard to imagine other options. Our decisions to buy or not to buy had been more destiny than decision.

A Spent Generation

Our baby-boomer parents were raised in fairly humble circumstances—a combination of lumberjacking, teaching, nursing homes, and auto repair. Through education, resourcefulness, and the benefits of a burgeoning economy, they worked their way into respected professions that led to middle-class success. But Nancy and I are of the generation after. Prosperous, post-World War II

America is the only reality we have known. While our parents and grandparents were shaped by the Great Depression of the 1930s and '40s, we were formed by the deceptive abundance of an unprecedented bull market in the 1980s and '90s. I have faint memories of waiting for gas in our family's wood-paneled Ford Country Squire station wagon during the mid-1970s oil embargo, but I have fresh and formative memories of millionaire secretaries at Microsoft and Internet start-ups like Amazon and eBay.

For our parents and grandparents, reminiscing about hard times in their formative years is based on real-life experience, but Nancy and I are more likely to put such reminiscing in the same category as Dana Carvey's grumpy old man character on *Saturday Night Live*. He says things like, "In my day, we didn't have *safety standards* for toys. We got rusty *nails* and big bags of *broken glass!* And that's the way it was, and we *liked* it! We *loved* it!" Neither of us had what I would describe as privileged childhoods, but we grew in the security of having our most basic needs met. We spent most our lives growing up in the middle of Maslow's hierarchy of needs, preoccupied with questions of love and belonging because, for the most part, we didn't have to worry about our basic safety and physical needs.

Our parents were raised one step removed from the farm and the land, but we were three and four steps removed. When we look at a map and see Otis Orchards listed just east of our home in Spokane, it doesn't immediately occur to us that at one time there were actually millions of fruit trees and hundreds of orchards filling the Spokane valley. When we drive Interstate 90 to Seattle, we don't readily make a connection between the infinite rows of green potato plants lining the freeway and the french fries the kids are munching on in the back seat. We've been shaped by a finely tuned marketplace where history and narrative are flattened into efficient commodities and feel-good brands.

Nancy grew up a few miles from the iconic Sherman Oaks Galleria from *Valley Girl* and *Fast Times at Ridgemont High*. She was among the first generation of children in Southern California who never mowed their own lawns or trimmed their hedges, let alone weeded a vegetable garden or cleaned out a chicken coop. My formative shopping mall was in a smaller, more nondescript setting in New Bern, North Carolina, but it had the distinction of being one of the first in the country, or so I was told. Probably every child upon their inaugural visit to the town's sprawling new shopping mall was told some such story. We were all in the vanguard of retail shopping in those days.

Nancy and I have lived the entirety of our married lives in the suburbs, safely surrounded by the chemically enhanced green lawns of the middle-income, two-kids, tree-lined-street life. We have never been prodigal in our consumption. We have always given 10 percent of our income to the church as a tithe, and we've always saved 10 percent of our income for retirement. We don't buy new cars—we're happy to troll the local auto auction for ten-year-old minivans. We don't have debt other than our mortgage. We've set aside money to contribute to our daughters' college educations. As of Christmas 2007, we thought we were doing everything right. We were dutiful consumers in the marketplace doing our responsible best, and yet there we were on December 27, worn out, angry, defensive, and disappointed.

Looking back, we could have easily chalked it all up to a bad case of the holiday blues, a seasonally induced bummer that would wear off when life got back to normal. But somehow the *Spa Factory Color Sparkle Custom Mix Nail Studio with Bonus* became a looking glass through which we began to see the need for significant change, not just during the Christmas season but for the whole year.

That night over pad thai we noticed that while we were at a loss for immediate answers, we were invigorated by the question itself: What could we do differently? The more we talked, the more it became obvious that we wanted to change more than our budget or our shopping habits. We wanted to break free of that hunger, that need for more. We were fed up with being stuck on autopilot and longed to be more intentional about what we bought and consumed. We wondered how we could make choices that had a positive impact on our friends and neighbors and community. We hoped for pathways that led to places of freedom and honest joy, as opposed to emotional standoffs in empty strip-mall parking lots.

As we finished our dinner and headed home, an idea started to take shape. We'd had a few recent experiences that seemed to share a common thread of satisfaction for us. The church where we serve as pastors, Millwood Presbyterian in Spokane, had started holding a farmers' market in the parking lot, and we enjoyed developing relationships with the farmers who fed us during the summer months. We'd planted a few vegetables in our garden as well and loved watching our girls discover how food comes from those tiny seeds. Even Christmas had given us a glimpse of how we might live differently—my sister had purchased all of our Christmas presents from local artisans in the suburbs of Sacramento where she lives. These random moments came together as a set of provocative proposals: What if we tried to limit our consumption to things that were local, used, homegrown, and homemade?

Then, in a fit of New Year's idealism, I proposed, "What if we did an experiment and tried to live by these rules for a whole year?"

The Rise of a Movement

Let me stop for a moment to comment on the whole "year-long experiment" phenomenon. In 2007, Barbara Kingsolver's book *Animal, Vegetable, Miracle*, in which she describes a year of eating local, was a bestseller. A couple in Vancouver, British Columbia, had recently completed a year following what they called "The 100-Mile Diet," eating only foods grown within a one-hundred-mile radius of their home, and their blog and book were getting a lot of attention. Julie Powell was cooking her way through Julia Child's cookbook and writing a blog describing her experience. That blog, of course, would soon be made into the best-selling book and Oscar-nominated movie, *Julie & Julia*.

Food projects have perhaps been most prominent on the cultural landscape, but the experiments in alternative consumption have been more diverse than that. The year 2007 also saw the publication of Sara Bongiorni's book *A Year Without "Made in China": One Family's True Life Adventure in the Global Economy*, and the year before that Judith Levine wrote *Not Buying It: My Year Without Shopping*. Colin Beavan, aka "No-Impact Man," was also wrapping up a year-long eco-experiment in 2007. As he put it, "For one year, my wife, my two-year-old daughter, my dog and I, while living in the middle of New York City, are attempting to live without making any net impact on the environment. In other words, no trash, no carbon emissions, no toxins in the water, no elevators, no subway, no products in packaging, no plastics, no air conditioning, no TV, no toilets."[1] His efforts were chronicled on a blog that was turned into a book and documentary movie.

So here I am writing a book about a year-long experiment, based in part on my blog, feeling not all that original and suspicious that we may be a couple years late to the party.

But in defense of our authenticity bona fides, I'm not an author. I have all of two newspaper editorials to my name. We didn't go into this as writers in search of a muse or as pastors looking for a way to become celebrities. And I can honestly say that we were unaware of these other experiments. We didn't say, "Let's do what Barbara Kingsolver did," or "Let's do a Christian version of *No Impact Man*." We'd never heard of a *locavore*, "someone who seeks to eat only locally grown food," nor did we know that the *Oxford English Dictionary* had announced a month before we hatched our plan that *locavore* was their word of the year for 2008. We had no clue as we transitioned to buying used, homegrown, and home-made that in a few months many would join us out of necessity as the economy suffered its worst collapse since the Great Depression.

In retrospect, this was a cultural moment that didn't need intentional awareness and connections or prescient predictions of economic peril. These experiments on the margins of our cultural marketplace, these aspirations toward a different consumption status quo, were bubbling up all over as if from a common hidden underground aquifer of unrest. In fact, the conversations and discoveries that awaited us had been brewing for decades.

Alice Waters opened her famous Chez Panisse restaurant in 1971 and has been working ever since to promote locally grown, seasonal foods. When Michelle Obama tore up a patch of White House lawn in 2009 to plant an organic garden, the media touted it as a culmination of Miss Waters's decades of food activism. Slow Food International was founded in the early '80s to promote good, clean, and fair food, and in 2008 this movement landed in our hometown of Spokane with a chapter dedicated to nurturing community around these food values.

Michael Pollan sums up these ongoing conversations and concerns in his best-selling book, *The Omnivore's Dilemma: A Natural History of Four Meals*. In 2008, the year of our experiment, Pollan's book was popping up as a required text on college freshman reading lists and holding steady on *The New York Times* bestseller list. Pollan starts out the book by describing food as a hub of contemporary issues. He writes, "'Eating is an agricultural act,' as Wendell Berry famously said. It is also an ecological act, and a political act, too. Though much has been done to obscure this simple fact, how and what we eat determines to a great extent the use we make of the world—and what is to become of it."[2]

More recently, the documentary *Food, Inc.* has taken this critique of industrial food and moved it into the mainstream, getting Oscar accolades and changing the way people eat along the way. Not a week goes by at the farmers' market that I don't hear someone say, "I saw the movie *Food, Inc.,* and I'll never eat the same again."

These conversations and movements have been more broadly about patterns of overconsumption and the ways in which our economic lives are out of whack. The phrase "voluntary simplicity" has been around since the early 1930s,[3] and in 1981 Duane Elgin popularized the concept with his book *Voluntary Simplicity: Toward a Way of Life That is Outwardly Simple, Inwardly Rich.* In the recently revised version of the book, Elgin describes the evolution of the idea of simple living since he first started speaking about the topic in the 1970s. He says, "Interest in sustainable ways of living has soared, and simplicity has moved from the margins of society to the mainstream. Simpler or greener approaches to living are becoming part of everyday life and culture."[4] The concept has gone from strange counter-culture to popular brand with a flagship magazine, *Real Simple,* and a TV show on TLC, *Real Simple, Real Life.*

Most recently Annie Leonard's book *The Story of Stuff: How Our Obsession with Stuff Is Trashing the Planet, Our Communities, and Our Health—And a Vision for Change* has summed up many of the movements and conversations that have sought to free us from the oppressive forces of "stuff" in our lives. She describes the hopeful trend of more and more people stepping off the treadmill of hyper-consumption, saying, "This approach—known variously as down-shifting, enough-ism, or voluntary simplicity—involves embracing a shift toward working and spending less. . . . Downshifters choose to prioritize leisure, community building, self-development, and health over accumulating more Stuff."[5]

Not surprisingly, the Christmas season has been a flash point for engaging these issues. In the early 1990s, social activists organized the first Buy-Nothing Day for the day after Thanksgiving to counteract the insanity of Black Friday and raise awareness of the issue of overconsumption. More recently a grass-roots movement called Advent Conspiracy has invited churches and communities to transform the consumption rhythms of the Christmas season. Their motto is "Worship Fully, Spend Less, Give More, Love All."

In 2008, Nancy and I were just getting our heads around the vocabulary of a changing culture: going green, carbon footprints, overconsumption, world poverty, microfinance, deforestation, reforestation, saving the planet, hybrid cars, composting food scraps, whole foods, free-range, fair trade, natural, organic, hormone free, cage free, backyard chickens, food not lawns, roundup ready, GMO, CAFO, rBST, walking school bus, bike-to-work week, buy local, buy less. Our personal journey was about to launch us into a cultural moment that had matured long before we came to the table.

Our entry into the fray reminds me of folks who come to me in my role as pastor with deep questions about God and the Bible. Upon discovering just a fraction of the thousands of volumes written and developed in response to their questions, they react with a wonderfully honest, "You mean someone has asked this question before?" I often feel like that around these issues of consumption—surprised and humbled that, for the most part, we had been oblivious to the determination and creativity of those who had already suggested profoundly meaningful answers to that question of how to live differently.

In light of the efforts of others' answers, it's fair to ask if the world really needs another book about one family's year-long consumption experiment. But I believe there are aspects of our modern marketplace that haven't already been unveiled and examined in other experiments.

A THEOLOGY OF PLENTY

I've found that one underexplored area of the conversation is the intersection of the Christian faith and these growing movements that rebel against the consumption status quo and seek to craft a more holistic and sustainable way of living.

A recent experience at Earth Day festivities in downtown Spokane is indicative of the need for more engagement from Christians and the church. It was a vibrant gathering of people, and it seemed like everyone in town was there. Local businesses and publications, colleges and grassroots organizations, they all had booths with signs and flyers and people eager to share their concern for the environment. Every major player in the life of the city was engaged with these pressing issues of our day. Everyone, that is, except the Christian church. There were no booths declaring that Jesus loves the earth, or that caring for creation is central to the Christian calling.

I'm not pointing fingers. My church wasn't there either, so I'm as much to blame as anyone. But that experience is a reminder to me that there is need for more open, thoughtful, and passionate engagement with these issues from people speaking with a distinctively Christian voice. With this book, I am joining a rising chorus in the church calling for Christians to be engaged with creation care and issues of consumption, not because they are popular, but because the Spirit of God is at work in the midst of these causes and concerns.

My assumption is that there is something unique that followers of Jesus have to offer the conversation. My hope in telling this story is that it will be a meaningful contribution to the ongoing effort to sort out faith in the midst of the choices of everyday life. At various points in the book this dimension of faith will be subtle and at other times more overt, but I want to be upfront in saying that our family's belief in Jesus as Lord and Savior and the rhythms of worship, prayer, and hope are the orienting center from which this story is told.

We didn't really formulate our year as a Christian endeavor, it simply was by nature of who we are. It was natural for us to inquire of our faith to help sort out new ways of being consumers in the world. Not unlike our experience of discovering long maturing conversations around local food and simple living, we were humbled and grateful to have our eyes opened to all kinds of uniquely Christian voices that were hidden in plain sight.

In 1977, Wendell Berry wrote *The Unsettling of America* in which he describes the American economic turn from nurturing the land to exploiting it. He has been a consistent and profound voice advocating for a local and sustainable way of life and has not been shy to explain that his perspectives arise out of his faith. For example, he once said:

> I take literally the statement in the Gospel of John that God loves the world. I believe that the world was created and approved by love, that it subsists, coheres, and endures by love, and that, insofar as it is redeemable, it can be redeemed only by love. I believe that divine love, incarnate and indwelling in the world, summons the world always toward wholeness, which ultimately is reconciliation and atonement with God. I believe that health is wholeness. For many years I have returned again and again to the work of the English agriculturist Sir Albert Howard who said, in *The Soil and Health*, that "the whole problem of health in soil, plant, animal and man [is] one great subject."[6]

For Berry, questions of faith and sustainability are inseparable. To take up the cause of caring for the earth is to take up the cause of Christ.

One of the first things Nancy did when we got home from Seattle was to get out one of her beloved cookbooks called *More With Less Cookbook*. I'd seen it around the house but had no idea that it was commissioned in the 1970s by the Mennonite Central Committee to help people: "There is a way of wasting less, eating less, and spending less which gives not less, but more."[7] The earthy recipes for spinach loaf and Navajo fry bread are interspersed with

Bible quotes and practical advice on how to live more simply. It's not unusual for churches to have cookbooks, but it was new to me to see how faith and food were seen as partners in the quest for a holy life.

And of course there are religious traditions in America that famously advocate for simple, sustainable living. The Hutterite settlements just a few miles to the west of Spokane have been pioneers of local sustainable living for decades. Seventh Day Adventists have always seen a life of healthy eating as part of a healthy faith. A 2010 Arizona State University study of Adventist vegetarians concludes that they are happier and healthier than omnivores.[8] The monastic traditions, most notably Benedict's Rule, are historical models of integrating faith and practice that are being explored in new ways outside the walls of the abbey. Jonathan Wilson-Hartgrove and Shane Claiborne are examples of fresh voices from this tradition, a new-monasticism for the modern world.

When I headed off to Fuller Seminary in 1991, I inherited a retired pastor's library of books. They had a 1970s patina and a musty, used-bookstore smell to match. The collection was a history lesson of trends in publishing for pastors in the second half of the twentieth century. The majority were either pragmatic advice for running a church or deep theological reflection. The philosophical abstractions of Tillich and Tournier were side by side with books such as *Leading Your Church to Growth* and *Strengthening the Adult Sunday School Class*. But there were others that spoke to the intersections of faith and consumption—Ron Sider's *Rich Christians in an Age of Hunger* and Tom Sine's *Mustard Seed Conspiracy*.

These integrated voices, where faith and consumption are envisioned as being caught up in the one drama of God's redemption, had been echoing around me for decades but for the first time our family was about to give them a proper hearing.

While our year-long experiment is not altogether unique in the cultural landscape, perhaps our reflection on faith in the midst of it offers a perspective worthy of being part of the conversation. That being said, I want to be careful not to give the wrong impression. Our intent is not to take a cultural narrative and shellac a Jesus fish on it. Hopefully this book is not like those T-shirts you buy at Christian bookstores that take a secular ad slogan and tweak it to sound all holy and righteous.

While faith is a central distinctive of this book, there is another aspect of our journey that we hope will add to the ever-expanding library of reports from the margins of the consumption status quo: we are ordinary. We set out to follow these rules while holding down two jobs, raising two children, and living absolutely ordinary lives in our ordinary neighborhood in our ordinary city.

We don't live in a large urban center like Manhattan or on an idyllic farm in the mountains of North Carolina. We live, like so many, in a middle-class suburb. When our kids show their chickens at the county fair, the other families ask us how many acres we have and we chuckle as we tell them about our house in a planned community with small lots, plastic fences, and deed restriction. I've been told that Spokane is often used by businesses to try out entrepreneurial initiatives because it is such an average, middle-of-the-road American city. It's in the "great-place-to-raise-a-family" category of cities and I love it for that.

So even though we were joining a movement in progress, in retrospect we can see that there was something different about an average Costco-shopping, YMCA-belonging, soccer-playing family entering into the strange confines of a year-long experiment that would come to involve plowing up the front yard and spending four hours looking for a birthday present.

THE RULE BOOK

After hatching our plan at the Thai restaurant we moved our little conspiracy-in-the-making to a Starbucks and wrote up our little manifesto on a green and white brochure titled, *We'd Love to Hear Your Thoughts.* We scribbled up a basic set of rules for shopping, which ironically included not going to Starbucks for an entire year. Here's what we came up with:

Local: We decided to buy goods from local producers, manufacturers, or growers, and we defined local as coming from eastern Washington and northern Idaho. We didn't have a precise mileage in mind. It was basically the outer limits from which our farmers from the church farmers' market traveled to sell goods in Spokane. We wanted to place value on things in a way that wasn't based solely on their price, forming a new economy of consumable goods anchored in caring relationships with people we know. In the end it seemed reasonable that we could nurture ongoing relationships in northern Idaho and eastern Washington. We agreed we would seek to do field trips to as many of these local producers as possible, meeting the people involved in bringing our goods to market, learning their way of life, their hopes and dreams and challenges.

The focus on local goods meant that there were many items, especially food, that would be limited by the Washington climate. Say good-bye to watermelon in January and hello to a long winter of lentils, peas, and potatoes.

Used: We would buy used products, preferably from one household to another. Craigslist and eBay would be our new shopping malls. Second-hand stores and garage sales would take on a whole new significance.

Homegrown: We had been novice gardeners, cultivating a small patch in our backyard for a few years. For the first time we would look to our yard as potential cropland, and our harvest as an essential component of our health and well being. The greenhouse I built the year before would now serve a vital purpose, allowing us to get an early start on our short growing season.

Homemade: Those things that weren't available by other means, we would seek to make at home. We agreed to allow some flexibility in buying the raw materials necessary to make the finished product, but we would try to get them from local sources. For example, when it came time to make our own ice cream, we bought cream from a local dairy but we settled on buying rock salt from a nonlocal source; when we ran out of vanilla we bartered with our neighbor to get what we needed.

Thailand: There was one major glitch in our newly emerging economy of local, used, homegrown, and homemade goods. The one food item we couldn't stomach giving up was coffee. While our Inland Northwest region is overrun with chicory, we had no interest in reliving the East German coffee crisis where they turned to a mixed brew of sugar beets, rye, and ground chicory roots. There are several quality roasters in the Spokane area, but we soon settled on the idea of choosing an international location from which we could buy select items during our year, including coffee. We crossed off Mexico and China from our list for obvious reasons and ultimately settled on Thailand where there is a marginal Arabica coffee industry but also the best Jasmine rice in the world. Nancy lived in Thailand for two years after graduating from college, which was invaluable as we sought to learn about the region and the people who live there, the economics of their lives, and how our consumption would impact them in positive and negative ways.

I know that might seem like a bit of a cop out—we'll buy local as long as we like what we can get. But there was more to our coffee decision than a mild addiction to caffeine. We'd heard people say that the best thing we Americans can do for impoverished countries is buy their goods. Our conspicuous consumption is the best thing to ever to happen to the third world, the logic goes, but as we stepped back from this we wondered if there weren't more meaningful ways to participate in the world economy. We discussed not wanting our experiment to be an abandonment of the world, as if we weren't among the fifty million richest people on the planet (47,380,750 to be exact, a top 1 percenter). We bear a global responsibility in a world where $2400 can buy a high-end flat screen TV at the Best Buy down the street from our house or schooling for an entire generation of school children in an Angolan village.[9]

Our goal was not to reject the economic realities of the world, but rather to enter them intentionally with eyes open to the impact of our purchases, even if it's just a can of tuna fish or pineapple, the majority of which we would learn originate in Thailand.

The rules at this point seemed to be writing themselves, one consistent wave of obvious and yet ridiculous notions that in a moment of grace seemed well within reach. In a final flourish we proposed that we would try to make a trip to Thailand as a family, just like we planned on making a field trip to the local flour mill and other local producers.

As we imagined putting all of our purchases through this new decision matrix we clarified some of the gray areas. We would allow ourselves to use everything in the house as of January 1. We would do our best to minimize the consumption of electricity, water, and fuel. I agreed to limit my use of the car by walking, taking the bus, carpooling, and biking. We would dine out only at locally owned restaurants and coffee shops—no large national or regional chain establishments. We agreed that we would be flexible when eating with others at a party or public event—no need to be snobby about it. We also agreed that we wouldn't make a big deal of our efforts. For one we didn't know if we could do it, but we also didn't want to give the impression that we thought everyone should follow our lead. We framed it as a personal journey to save ourselves, not a crusade to save the world.

The point of all of this was relatively simple. We wanted to step back from the cultural passion for consumption that led us to want the new and next thing. We wanted to break free of the belief that our hope and joy could be found in consumable goods. In our small way, we hoped to minimize our contribution to a disposable society in which anything that has lost the shine of newness has outlived its usefulness. On a more personal level, we wanted to raise our daughters as children of the kingdom of God, not the kingdom of goods. We wanted to live more fully integrated lives by making financial decisions based on what we value and believe. We wanted to find more joy in the everydayness by slowing down, being intentional with our time and resources, and building meaningful relationships in our community. We didn't know if our experiment would accomplish any of those things when we set out, but we knew something had to change.

Who would have guessed an overpackaged teeny-bopper manicure set could throw our entire way of life into question? As ridiculous as our prospective year of consumption seemed, that night we wondered if it wasn't our middle-class American way of life that had become ridiculous. All it took is one question, "How could we do it differently?" Nancy and I went to bed that night with a sense of anticipation and no real way of knowing if our wild speculations would come to fruition. If so, we had some preparations to make. January 1 was three days away.

I: Winter

In a paradox, opposites do not negate each other—they cohere in a mysterious unity at the heart of reality. Deeper still, they need each other for health, as my body needs to breathe in as well as breathe out. But in a culture that prefers the ease of either/or thinking to the complexities of paradox, we have a hard time holding opposites together. We want light without darkness, the glories of spring and summer without the demands of autumn and winter.[1]

—Parker Palmer

Bless the LORD, O my soul.
* O LORD my God, you are very great.*
You are clothed with honor and majesty,
* wrapped in light as with a garment.*
You stretch out the heavens like a tent,
* you set the beams of your chambers on the waters,*
you make the clouds your chariot,
* you ride on the wings of the wind. . . .*
You cause the grass to grow for the cattle,
* and plants for people to use,*
to bring forth food from the earth,
* and wine to gladden the human heart,*
oil to make the face shine,
* and bread to strengthen the human heart.*
The trees of the LORD are watered abundantly,
* the cedars of Lebanon that he planted.*
In them the birds build their nests;
* the stork has its home in the fir trees.*

The high mountains are for the wild goats;
   the rocks are a refuge for the coneys.
You have made the moon to mark the seasons;
   the sun knows its time for setting. . . .
These all look to you
   to give them their food in due season;
when you give to them, they gather it up;
   when you open your hand, they are filled with good things.
When you hide your face, they are dismayed;
   when you take away their breath, they die
   and return to their dust.
When you send forth your spirit, they are created;
   and you renew the face of the ground.
      —Ps. 104:1-3, 14-19, 27-30 (NRSV)

NORMAL PEOPLE WOULD PLAN MONTHS IN ADVANCE FOR an experiment like this. Perhaps they would start in spring with the hopeful appearance of asparagus sprigs and onion shoots. That was the approach Barbara Kingsolver and her family took as they began their *Animal, Vegetable, Miracle* experiment. And even if someone were to think about launching such an experiment in the dead of winter, they would be wise to spend all summer canning and freezing every bit of fresh fruits and vegetables they could get their hands on. They would buy a cow's worth of beef and pack it in the freezer like an Inuit preparing for a long, hard winter. And knowing that anything in the house at the beginning of the year is fair game, the smart people among us would go into the year with a well-stocked house complete with subconsciously stowed items like twenty-pound bags of sugar and a year's supply of toilet paper awaiting feigned discovery once the experiment got started.

We put in two days of casual preparation.

True, Nancy did make a covert trip to the store to stock up on chocolate chips and toilet paper. When she asked me what we should do to prepare, I naively said we'd be fine. "That's all part of the adventure isn't it? We'll take each day as it comes." Needless to say, the days came quickly. Once we crossed the threshold of the new year, we were forced to face the harsh reality of two cups of sugar in the pantry and twenty sheets of paper in the printer, not to mention the limits of January produce.

It might not have made much sense from a planning perspective, but there was a certain logic to starting in the dead of winter. Having devised our plans and plotted our course, the rhythm of our first days was to slow down and wait, to wait for the ground to thaw out and for the days to get longer. There was no getting around this seasonal brick wall. Those first days were not unlike the weekly rhythm of the Sabbath day.

We tend to imagine the Sabbath as a time of rest at the end of a long week, a time to recharge batteries and gear up for another crazy week. Indeed, in the Jewish observation it has always been the seventh day, the last day of the week. But it's important to take note that in the book of Genesis, the Sabbath is creation's seventh day, but for humankind it is the first full day. As the story goes man and woman are created and commissioned. "Be fruitful and increase in number; fill the earth and subdue it. Rule over the fish of the sea and the birds in the sky and over every living creature that moves on the ground" (Gen. 1:28). It is a comprehensive call to productivity and action, the ultimate pep talk.

Imagine awaking for this first day with the longest to-do list ever devised hanging on the fridge and God says, "First we rest." Genesis says, "Thus the heavens and the earth were completed in all their vast array. By the seventh day God had finished the work he had been doing; so on the seventh day he rested from all his work. Then God blessed the seventh day and made it holy, because on it he rested from all the work of creating that he had done" (Gen.

2:1-3). The Hebrew word *shabbat* literally means "stop." The first full day in creation for man and woman was not a day of work, but a day of stopping and waiting. The rhythm of the Sabbath starts in the goodness and reality of God as creator, the lord of all things and all people. We are born into the grace of a world we didn't create, sustained by provisions we didn't stockpile, and encouraged to rest in our utter dependence.

I've always found it curious that in the first Genesis creation account the creative energies of each day are summed up with the words, "And there was evening, and there was morning . . ." In the same way that the Sabbath is first and not last, this order of evening and morning confuses our normal way of thinking. We imagine morning as the beginning of a new day. We tend to see our waking to action as the beginning place but the rhythm of creation puts the evening first. The wisdom of the Jewish observation of the Sabbath has always been to follow this pattern, starting not at sunup but at sundown. The day begins not with taking charge, but rather with letting go in the vulnerability of darkness and sleep.

This practice was revised in the Christian tradition with the resurrection of Jesus. The sun breaking forth in the morning became the central image of the newly conceived Lord's Day on Sundays. Easter sunrise became the high holy event of the year. But even in the Christian tradition, the triumph of Easter is not first but last. First there are forty days of waiting and hoping in the darkness of the season of Lent; like forty years in the wilderness, the wisdom of the journey is to begin in darkness. When the light does come and we awake, we enter a world that is, above all, a gift, a theater of God's grace.[2]

To start in January did not feel like a gift of grace initially, but looking back I can see how it might have been a key to us actually sticking with our plans. Had we launched quickly into the hard work of summer, we would have likely worn ourselves out in a flurry of activity. Our enthusiasm would have gotten the better of us, and, like the vast majority of New Year's resolutions, our efforts would have crumbled under the weight of our limited discipline and energy. The dark days of January forced us to settle in for the long haul.

For fear that I may be in danger of romanticizing the virtues of these first days, I want to highlight one more aspect of starting in winter that is reminiscent of the Sabbath; it was a total pain in the butt, an inconvenience of epic proportions. As Judith Shulevitz describes in her book, *Sabbath World*, "The old-time Sabbath does not fit comfortably into our lives. It scowls at our dewy dreams of total relaxation and freedom from obligation. The goal of the Sabbath may be rest, but it isn't personal liberty or unfettered leisure. The Sabbath seems designed to make life as inconvenient as possible."[3]

CHAPTER 2

Food with a Face on It

For some time now I have been troubled by the seeming disappearance of any robust alternative to the pervasive culture of late capitalism, whether in the church or in the society at large. We are drowning in a flood of consumer goods and are drenched in showers of media images. We live in a smorgasbord of culture in which everything is interesting and nothing really matters. We have lost a vision of the good life, and our hopes for the future are emptied of moral content. Instead of purposefully walking to determinate places, we are aimlessly floating with random currents.[1]
—Miroslav Volf

For the entire law is fulfilled in keeping this one command: "Love your neighbor as yourself."
—Gal. 5:14

THERE WERE MANY THINGS TO BE SORTED OUT AS WE began filtering our lives through these four rules: local, used, homegrown, and homemade. The most pressing question during our first days was, "What are we going to eat?"

One of our first phone calls was to Greenbluff, a nearby collective of farms on the ridge overlooking the prairie just north of our house. It's the kind of place you take your kids to for harvest festivals with pumpkin-shaped jumpy castles and corn mazes. A friend calls it "food tourism." Just as people go to the zoo to look at the animals, city folk can go to places like Greenbluff to look at the farms and farmers on display. But they aren't just for show. They are real farms and in January, when all the leaves have dropped from the trees in the orchards and the school buses have made their final field trips, there is a remnant of the season's harvest still waiting in the fields. We got a tip that one of the farms, Siemers's, had some winter squash left over.

When Nancy called the farm, we didn't get a customer service representative or the produce department manager. To our delight, Mr. Siemers himself greeted us with a friendly, "Hello."

The rumor was true: while Mr. Siemers had pretty much shut things down for the season, he seemed enthusiastic about having us come out to look over what he had left. We had been experiencing record cold and snow in Spokane, and when we arrived at the farm, patches of thick ice covered the bare, frozen fields of Mr. Siemers's twenty acres.

Our new farmer friend greeted us in his driveway, and as we walked toward his small retail shop, I noticed a large, four-story castle in the middle of his cornfield. The texture of the chip board could be seen through the Renaissance inspired murals that covered the castle walls. It was only a couple months earlier that the girls and I climbed to the top of the structure having successfully navigated the corn maze that surrounded it. We got the package deal that included a trip through the maze, a ride on the make-shift train that followed the path of well-worn figure eights around the farm, and a small pumpkin from the pumpkin patch. I remember thinking it was odd that they had signs throughout the maze warning us not to touch the large ears of corn protruding from the tall stalks. It seemed like they had gone to so much trouble to create an experience for people that the corn was more prop than crop.

But apparently every ear of corn was important in their economic scheme of farming. As I would soon discover, this was more true that I could have imagined.

When we stepped into the small store with mostly empty shelves and a small cash register, we were excited to see that Mr. Siemers had an abundance of winter squash. And it wasn't just common varieties like acorn and butternut. He had some of the most exotic, glorious squash I had ever seen. They were bulging and deformed—more like garden creatures than food. They were crusty and barnacled, colored like rainbows in muted earthy tones. There was delicate squash that looked like it was wearing an orange, green, and yellow striped prison jumpsuit, and knobby turban squash that looked like Kane from the *Alien* movie with a minisquash pushing its way out of the belly of the larger host. There were thirty-pound pink banana squash the size and shape of a large wiener dog, and the notorious giant blue hubbards that my friend says are so tough he uses an axe and chops them up like kindling for his wife to prepare in the kitchen. It was like I had walked into the vegetable equivalent of the Tatooine cantina in *Star Wars*, full of grotesque and fascinating characters.

When we piled up our bounty at the small cash register, Mr. Siemers was a little surprised to find us so enthusiastic and complimentary of winter squash, usually the poor stepchild of the vegetable world. So he took us out back to the barn and showed us huge stacks of wooden crates full of several tons of orange-fleshed globes. I mentioned how impressed I was with his stockpile, and he said with resignation, "Yeah, all of this is going to rot. It's too cold in here for it to keep through the winter."

It was hard for me to imagine working so hard through the heat and dust of summer, dodging early and late frosts, heavy rains, and surprising hail storms to finally bring crops into the store house, only to have them rot. Mr. Siemers went on to offer a farmer's lament, explaining that it's not easy to make it as a farmer these days. Now I understood the urgent, "Do not touch the corn," signs in the corn maze. Mr. Siemers was not P. T. Barnum of the ag world. He was just a farmer trying to sort out a business model for growing corn. Large fields of corn were apparently not so profitable without large faux castles in the middle of them.

PRODUCE OR PRODUCT?

With our car listing to the rear under the weight of our winter supply of starch, we ventured ten miles from Greenbluff to the grocery store to see what locally sourced items they might have for sale. If you ever want to waste an afternoon in utter confusion, walk the aisles of a store with one question: "Where did this food come from?" It's like being an investigator in an episode of CSI, trying to read the nuances and hints of food labels, hoping for trace evidence. Labels are dedicated to corporate offices that have no relation to the journey of the food in the package. Or they proudly announce, "Product of U.S.A." as if food were a T-shirt or piece of furniture. Sometimes, as in the case of a certain brand of apple juice, they say, "Product of the U.S.A." with "Product of China" printed directly beneath it. Does it count as local apple juice if it's laced with ascorbic acid from China?

Thankfully, products from Thailand were fair game, so we stocked up on tuna fish, pineapple, and Jasmine rice. We compromised our coffee standards with some locally roasted—but not grown—coffee beans in the hopes that we would soon figure out how to acquire Thai coffee beans. I got a six-pack of one of the few regional microbrew beers. And we found, after a little investigating, a supply of local lentils and dried beans. We would soon learn that almost all the flour on the store shelves is from the area we'd mapped out as our local "foodshed." It turns out that the Inland Northwest is one of is one of the most prolific wheat-producing regions in the world, which is probably why there is a major pasta manufacturer in Spokane—a fact for which we were profoundly grateful. We found marinara sauce made in Spokane by an Italian woman. We figured that since it was for sale in the store, it had to be safe, even though the simple label on the jar made it look like it had been cooked up on the stove top in her home kitchen.

Our shopping cart looked like we'd just gone through the line at the local food bank. It was full of random samplings of whatever happened to fit our criteria rather than a cart filled with staples and actual meals. It wasn't a gourmet's delight, but we were almost certain we'd found enough to feed ourselves. We could rest in the knowledge that we wouldn't starve, although scurvy, something I'd never imagined apart from fifteenth century shipping adventures, seemed like a remote possibility.

The produce section offered pretty slim pickings with most of the fruits and vegetables coming from California and Arizona. At the end of one aisle, I noticed a display of butternut squash. Compared to the beauties we'd seen rotting in Mr. Siemers' barn, these squash looked skinny and malnourished. I picked one up and read the sticker with disbelief: "Product of Mexico." For the first time in my life, I felt like booing the produce manager at a grocery store.

It's as hard to trace the exact origin of a butternut squash from Mexico as it is one that's stamped "Product of the U.S.A." But the trade routes of Mexican-grown produce are well-worn enough to speculate with some precision. Butternut squash from Mexico is available year-round with its peak season running October through June. In January, the supply routes go further south to places like El Carrizo in the Sinaloa region where the brown jagged hills of the desert give way to the green geometry of irrigated factory farms.

The squash in the store in Spokane was grown in fields that require the extensive use of fossil-fuel-based fertilizers and pesticides along with copious amounts of water—a scarce commodity in those parts of Mexico. Once it was ripe, this squash was harvested by farmhands making close to the minimum wage, which in 2007 in the Sinaloa region was 47.60 pesos per day (about four American dollars for one day of work). Assuming regular work and good health, these men and women would have made a little over $1,000 for a year's labor, likely much less because of the seasonal nature of the job.

Once it left the field, the squash was loaded onto a truck that used one gallon of gas for every seven miles traveled. It was shipped 680 miles north through the Sonoran desert to Nogales, Arizona, where it was loaded onto another truck and shipped an additional 1500 miles to Spokane, Washington. There, it made its way onto the shelves of my local grocery store and into my incredulous hands, more than 2,000 miles from its point of origin and with close to 400 gallons of diesel fuel expended for the journey. All of this when just ten miles away in Greenbluff, Mr. Siemers had a barn full of far superior, locally grown squash that was going to waste.

I couldn't help but ask, "What's going on here?!"

WAKING UP

Going into this year, I thought I was a fairly enlightened consumer. I wasn't caught up in some mad dash to compete with the Joneses or obsessed with brands and status and climbing the ladder of success. On the other hand, I wasn't at all uncomfortable with the economics of everyday life. I liked the convenience of taking the kids to McDonald's even if I hated the nutritional content and feared the ongoing bacterial experiment going on in the tunnels of the PlayPlace. I couldn't imagine life without two cars and the freedom and immediacy of being able to get behind the wheel at any moment to get a Slurpee at the local 7-Eleven. As much as I struggled with the generic predictability of the "master planned" neighborhoods we had lived in for years, that inherent sameness was part of the appeal, part of the security. Our houses came with fairly stable market values and some assurances that our neighbors wouldn't stack their lawns with El Caminos.

Truth be told, I wanted a fence between me and my neighbors, and I wanted a garage full of my own power tools and lawn mower. When given the choice between life served family style, with the anxiety of wondering if there would be any metaphorical Kung Pao chicken left by the time the plate came to me, I had chosen the life served in safely compartmentalized portions. This was my comfort zone.

That isn't to say I didn't have my moments of awareness and wondering about the justice of this whole web of consumption. Several months before we launched our experiment, I was leading a men's Bible study on the book of James, and we came across a passage under the foreboding title, "Warning to Rich Oppressors." It read, "You have hoarded wealth in the last days. Look! The wages you failed to pay the workers who mowed your fields are crying out against you. The cries of the harvesters have reached the ears of the Lord Almighty. You have lived on earth in luxury and self-indulgence. You have fattened yourselves in the day of slaughter. You have condemned and murdered the innocent one, who was not opposing you" (Jas. 5:3-6).

I asked our group, "How do we know who the rich oppressors are today? We live in a world of far-flung industrial practices where everything is a commodity and we have no idea of where and out of what conditions our consumer goods have emerged. So how do we know for sure that we're not the rich oppressors? How do we know that James isn't talking about us?"

This last question haunted me long after our group discussed the implications of James's warning. *How do we know?* I wondered. *Is it possible that the person who sewed together my shirt was some kind of indentured worker? Is it possible that the farmer who grew the coffee beans I used to brew my morning dose of caffeine was exploited by an unscrupulous buyer and left destitute? What are the conditions of the chickens that laid the eggs that were sitting on my breakfast plate? What is in that sausage, and how did it get there?* And while I can live without knowing about the sausage, these are the kind of questions that stuck with me, even if they didn't move me to action.

Somehow standing there holding a butternut squash in my hand turned me from a curious observer with occasional consumer indigestion to being an active participant, indignant that I'd never really noticed that local farmers were dying on the vine while we exploited poor people in Mexico and burned up forty millennia worth of stored energy like it was nothing, all so I could save ten cents a pound on my squash.

A local farmer recently said to me, "Thanks for being a food activist." I'd never really thought of myself as an activist of any kind, but if I am, my life as an advocate and campaigner and cheerleader for local farmers started in the produce section of the grocery store with Mr. Siemers's barn full of rotting squash heavy on my heart.

Just a few days into our year these rules had turned the tables on me, reading and revealing me. They were doing a work of holy mischief in my life, turning the disconnected, isolated objects of my consumer life into an inseparable web of meanings and realities. I was learning that it takes more than a Bible study and discussion to go from an observer to an activist. I was learning that it takes a rule for living, a confined space, with meaningful and intentional constraints, to form me as a responsible citizen in God's creation. It wasn't in imagining the abstract holiness of God that I would find my way, but rather by paying attention to the world around me, a world that is covered in God's fingerprints, a world that reveals the conspiracy of God's kingdom in the details of everyday living. In the words of Clemens Sedmak, "Theology is about waking up. . . . [W]aking up is about going to the root of matters . . . and is part of living a responsible life."[2]

The Farmer at the Table

In the early 1970s some folks in Japan responded to the decline of small farms and concerns about food safety by creating direct relationships between farmers and eaters. Instead of going to the grocery store, they went directly to the producers to get their milk, vegetables, and fruit. While there were similar programs popping up elsewhere at that time, the Japanese system was unique in the word *teikei* they use to describe it. Literally translated it means "relationship" or "partnership," but the innovators of the program describe it as meaning "food with the farmer's face on it."[3] In the 1980s similar programs emerged in America and are commonly called CSA or Community Supported Agriculture programs. This usually means you sign up to get a weekly box of veggies and farm-fresh food in exchange for buying a subscription or share from the farmer for the growing season.

I personally think CSA is a dreadful term for such a cool arrangement. I much prefer calling it "food with the farmer's face on it." That says it all to me. Even more exciting would be to put the faces of your farmer's whole family on your food.

One of the reasons the number of small farmers has declined is that it's not easy to make a living with all the inherent risks of the marketplace, not to mention the climate. The great thing about signing up for a "food with the farmer's face on it" program is that you become partners with a farm family, giving them a steady source of income while getting a steady source of quality produce.

People ask me about the best part of our experiment, and it's definitely the relationships we've developed with the people who bring our food to market. We've gone from shoppers who were primarily self-interested in our consumption, to an experience where we feel like partners in a community of consumption and provision. We've got faces on our veggies now. (You can find a farmer who offers a CSA program in your area at localharvest.org.)

When I first wrote about CSA on our blog, a reader sent me this comment about her family's experience of opening up their first CSA box of the season. This family lives in the Sacramento area, so they have items in their box you might not have in your area. She wrote:

> We're joining you in spirit today (if even just a little bit). We picked up our first box from our local CSA. It was nice to see that the farm is more what you would expect from a working farm, and not as sanitized as the picture-perfect flyer. We brought our big box home and it was like opening a present. I think the kids were surprised to see lettuce that didn't come in a plastic bag and I was surprised to cut up garlic that was moist and fresh. (You mean you don't have to peel off the hard, stale part before you chop it up?)
>
> In our box we got a few varieties of garlic and onions, small yellow tomatoes, basil, spinach, kale, pea shoots, bib lettuce, red lady apples, oranges, satsumas, and the tastiest little honeydew melons. We made a salad, pasta with lots of veggies and it was all very tasty! It's fun to have to find recipes to use the veggies in. Does anyone have a good Kale recipe? I can't wait to see what we get next week!

For us and for so many people who participate in CSA, the bounty of produce is only part of the benefit of owning a share of a farmer's crop. The real beauty comes from building a connection with the person who feeds your family. At first glance, our rules for the year seem a little random. And when we initially wrote them out, they were based on intuitive hunches more than an overarching philosophy. But it quickly became clear to us that there was a consistent ethic to our rules, one even we couldn't have articulated until we started trying to live it out. That ethic has to do with relationships.

This became clear to me a couple of months into the year when we were invited to speak to graduate and undergraduate students at Washington State University who were studying sustainable agriculture and global food systems. I felt a little bit like Leonardo DiCaprio in the movie *Catch Me if You Can*, where he goes around pretending to be a doctor and a pilot, and people inexplicably believe him. I pretended to have something meaningful to say about local and global food systems and we ended up having a great dialogue. When the professor, Dr. Jussaume, asked me about our guiding principles, he said, "So in describing your experience you've mentioned the importance of your connections to farmers but you've also talked about sticking to eastern Washington and northern Idaho. What is it that's guiding you? Is it geography or is it people?"

Without hesitating I said, "Really from the beginning it's been about nurturing relationships with people. We started out the year saying we want to know the people we are buying food and other items from. We had this naive thought that if we could develop these relationships and be committed to caring for these people in an actual relationship that somehow we would become more responsible in our consumption and as a result more human and more faithful."

As was the case for most of our work integrating faith in the midst of what we were learning, I stumbled into a realization while the words were coming out of my mouth: "In my Christian tradition we are guided by the great commandment to love our neighbor as ourselves. We have found that when it comes to so many things we buy and consume that we are disconnected from our neighbors, and therefore disconnected from our responsibility to love them. The geography is a means to an end. It puts us in proximity to people and makes relationships possible. It makes love possible."

Two weeks into our experiment, after tracking down the squash at Siemers Farm and a bunch of other items from local farmers, we sat down around the dinner table and lowered our heads to pray as we always do. We predictably thanked God for the food, but then our prayers spontaneously went into uncharted territory, thanking God for the farmers and producers. We thanked God for Mr. Siemers and prayed for his struggles and the injustices in the marketplace that allow his crops to rot. We thanked God for Mrs. Tulia who made our spaghetti sauce. (We hadn't met her yet but at least her picture was on the jar and she only lived five miles away.) Our prayer became an inventory not just of the food but of the people whose work had gone into producing it. Every food item on our plates was connected to a person we knew, a person who was sorting out a life of hopes and dreams and struggles. These were our neighbors, and that night, through our prayers, we were able to love them like never before.

CHAPTER 3

A Beautiful Catastrophe

The world of efficiency ignores both loves, earthly and divine, because by definition it must reduce experience to computation, particularity to abstraction, and mystery to a small comprehensibility. Efficiency, in our present sense of the world, allies itself inevitably with the machinery, as Neil Postman demonstrates in his useful book Technopoly. *"Machines," he says, "eliminate complexity, doubt, and ambiguity. They work swiftly, they are standardized, and they provide us with numbers that you can see and calculate with." And yet love obstinately answers that no loved one is standardized. A body, love insists, is neither a spirit nor a machine; it is not a picture, a diagram, a chart, a graph, an anatomy; it is not an explanation; it is not a law. It is precisely and uniquely what it is. It belongs to the world of love.*[1]

—Wendell Berry

SOMEWHERE IN THE DEVELOPMENT OF SUBURBAN LIFE AND culture, birthday parties became a kind of annualized debutante ball complete with the all-important theme. And the catch is that the particular theme for any given year is determined by the random synapses of seven-year-olds, whose ability to differentiate between reality and fantasy is rather fluid. When my daughter Lily says she wants a jungle theme for her bedroom, I sort of get that, but when she says she wants an actual tree in the middle of her room that she can swing from, she loses me. Still, when children say they want something for their birthdays, the pressure to deliver is on.

So it's no wonder that when faced with planning Noel's eighth birthday party in early January, our collective anxiety level went through the roof. Just when we had resolved to step off the crazy consumption treadmill, we had to negotiate the sensitive territory of our daughter's (and our) expectations for a great birthday party. Until then we had lived in the world of "everything is possible," where with a few mouse clicks and phone calls we could buy a High School Musical (HSM) cake at Safeway, a piñata that looks just like Zach Efron, HSM favor boxes, that HSM bedding set Noel had been wishing for, and enough processed junk food to make even the pickiest princess happy. But we had moved into a world of constraints. Every birthday decision—from the cake we would eat, to the decorations we could buy, to the food we would serve—would have to pass through our grid of rules. Next to Christmas, birthday parties are a parent's greatest consumerist nightmare, and this was an early test of our resolve and commitment. Would we make an exception or would we stick with it?

Adventures in Gift Giving

With a week to go until Noel's party, we found ourselves facing a trial run for these new constraints as they related to birthday parties: Noel was invited to the birthday party of an eight-year-old boy and we needed to buy a gift. We put this purchasing decision through our local, used, homegrown, or homemade matrix and came up with . . . nothing. As we considered the options, Nancy and I were acutely aware of that hallowed time at parties where hordes of kids gather around the birthday boy or girl and everything grows solemn and silent while the presents are opened. One by one, wrapped packages are handed to the birthday child and the identity of the gift giver is announced to the hushed audience. Everyone looks at the gift giver almost as much as they look at the gift receiver. The pressure is intense: How will the birthday child respond? Will he love it? Will the gift get a lukewarm, half-hearted reception? Will the other kids be jealous or will they snicker?

In reality, the patterns of consumption are so well worn with these rituals that there is very little risk of social exile. We all go to the same stores and wander the same rows of toys, and the kids all point to some variation of the same plastic assemblage made in China that will soon be at the bottom of the toy bin or broken or in the large plastic bag with donations to the Goodwill. The excitement of the new toys will wear out, and the kids will move on, never really remembering the exchange.

But now the danger of social isolation seemed like a real possibility. We were discovering that stepping out of the consumer mainstream was not something we could just contain within our household as an isolated experiment. By nature, our consuming choices have tentacles that unknowingly attach us to one another. The gift decision caused us to see these connections anew.

The night before the birthday party, the pressure was mounting. We still didn't have a gift for this boy. Nancy kept asking me what we were going to do, until I finally agreed to do something I'd never done before. I would step into unfamiliar parenting territory and help shepherd Noel through the process of selecting a present for her friend.

Early the next morning we climbed in the car and headed to Coeur d'Alene, Idaho, about a half an hour away. We knew of a small shopping district in the city that features the wares of local artisans. Instead of feeling like we had another boring errand to run, the girls and I shared a sense of adventure as we hit the freeway.

As we strolled from shop to shop, it didn't take long to confront the two major metrics that normally determine the selection of an elementary-age birthday present: price and time. In a life crammed with soccer practices, piano lessons, committee meetings, and yard work, there isn't much time for buying presents so the ability to swoop in and out of a Walgreens or Walmart is a boon to busy families—at least it had been to us. It's the 15:15 rule of birthday presents: 15 minutes and $15 dollars. But we had already spent thirty minutes in the car just to get to a store. Noel was having a difficult time wrapping her imagination around the options. She wasn't used to considering the comparative merits of a fabricated metal salmon silhouette on a magnet and a small blown-glass frog. And I was having a hard time finding anything that cost $15.

After wandering through all the stores and with Noel still undecided, we stopped by a local, family-owned burger joint, Hudson's Hamburgers. They only have bar seating and you order your food one burger or piece of pie at a time. It has the feel of the food counter at an old Woolworth's five-and-dime store or an old donut shop where the town elders gathered around chatting about the day's news. After standing for a while waiting for stools to open up, we sat down, ordered our burgers, and shook off our frustrations. We were now a good two hours into our task, but the fresh pie and the joy of sitting on rotating stools took the edge off.

With our stomachs full, we retraced our steps. Noel finally settled on a small, smoothly honed, handcrafted wooden puzzle box, the kind that opens up when you pulled out a lever. It even had a secret compartment. It was just the kind of thing I would have liked when I was eight years old, which made it a little less painful to fork over $30 for it. It also helped to know the box was one of a kind. It included a business card of the craftsman in Spokane who made it. Our rules said we wanted to meet the people who made the things we purchased, so on the drive back home we called the man on the card to introduce ourselves and explain that we had just purchased one of his wonderful boxes. He was an older gentleman with a gruff voice and a bit of a paranoid demeanor. I asked him if we could stop by sometime and visit with him. After asking for clarification several times about what exactly we wanted from him, he said good-bye and hung up. Apparently, this whole closing-the-gap and connecting-in-relationships business was going to take adjustments on both sides of the transaction.

When Noel got back from the birthday party later in the afternoon, I eagerly asked her how her friend liked the puzzle box. She said, "It was his favorite present. After he opened all the gifts, he played with my present. I think he was hiding his little soldier in the secret compartment. Thanks Dad." We paid twice the money and spent four hours instead of fifteen minutes, but it was worth it. Noel would remember what she got her friend, unlike all the other fancy hunks of cheap plastic she'd handed over at parties, and she would remember time with her dad. I'd like to think that this experience made her a better friend, one who is better equipped to care for people, whether they are the ones who make the gifts or the ones who receive them.

Of course, living out this experiment didn't always sit so well with the girls—or with us for that matter. We had our first mini-rebellion shortly before Noel's party. Something triggered Lily to yell with gusto that she was "sick of this local stuff." It didn't help that I had refused to buy her a corn dog at the grocery store earlier in the day, but after she settled down she explained that she was frustrated it took so long to shop for food. She had been shaped by all those years of sweeping in and sweeping out of the grocery store, following the path of least resistance to the checkout stand.

We knew this experiment was going to shake up our shopping habits, but it was turning into a great exercise in parenting as well. It wasn't so much about our particular set of rules but about having any set of official rules and working together to be faithful to them.

We had a very tangible way of sharing in a common commitment. This was a fresh experience for me as a parent.

We've always had rules. The other day I said I wanted something, and my daughter said, "Don't say I want," because Nancy is constantly reminding them to say, "May I please have?" instead of "I want." That's one of our rules. But we'd never had explicit rules like the ones we were working with during that year. They were frustrating at times, for all of us, but there was something beautiful in the way they bound us together.

Our rules often reminded me of the tradition of formal Rules in monastic communities, like the Rule of St. Benedict. Benedict talks about the rules as the instruments of "the spiritual art" and the monastery as the "workshop in which we perform all these works with diligence."[2] I began to see our rules as instruments of the familial art, and our house as a sort of workshop in which we were creating something together.

THE FAMILY FLAMINGO

Having navigated the first real test of our resolve with the help of the birthday box and having averted Lily's small mutiny, we had to sort out our plans for Noel's birthday party. There were two major projects that loomed large: Nancy was going to make a birthday cake from scratch, and I was going to help the kids make a piñata.

After some research online, Noel decided she wanted to make a flamingo piñata. This involved two spheres, a large one for the body and another smaller one for the head, all connected together by a long cardboard neck made from the rigid center of a roll of wrapping paper and two tube legs made from toilet-paper rolls taped together. We found a recipe for the plaster using just flour and water. Instead of going to the store to buy supplies, we combed the house to find the raw materials that would serve our purposes. Fortunately we had what we needed.

The day before the party, we cut up strips of newspapers and magazines, blew up balloons, mixed up a batch of floury goo, and went about the marvelous work of covering the balloons with layer upon layer of plastered strips of paper. The girls loved squeezing the slime through their fingers and I was enjoying the engineering challenge of how to get this awkward, top-heavy beast to stand on two legs. After two hours of fine tuning our creature we propped it up to dry for the night, cleaned up the mess, and went to bed early, tired from managing our small manufacturing operation.

In the middle of the night I heard a great crash and upon investigating found our flamingo crumpled on the floor like a bird that had flown into a window. I stood there feeling the terror of this uncharted territory, like Lucille Ball supervising the conveyor belt of chocolates when everything goes haywire. It was a position of discomfort with which I would become familiar over the course of the year. I patched together our mutilated flamingo carcass and went to bed, muttering that $10 piñatas from Mexico were one of capitalism's most underappreciated gifts to parents across the land.

The next morning was B-day. We woke up and the girls and I eagerly checked the progress of our flamingo. Our design called for the candy to go in the large balloon-shaped body with the head serving as decoration, but our design had a flaw. We were a little too industrious with our layers of papier-mache and it wasn't drying quickly enough. We got out the hair dryers and tried to speed up the process, but running short on time and still needing to decorate the bird and take care of the other party details, we threw caution to the wind and got out the needle to pop the balloons.

It was our moment of truth. Noel poked into the bulbous torso and as the balloon slowly deflated, the wet walls of the papier-mache stuck to the balloon, pulling inward like a little universe collapsing on itself. With only an hour till her friends arrived, Noel was distraught to see her prized piñata looking like a like a crushed tin can.

She said, "Daddy, what are we going to do? Daddy," and she went racing out of the room with tears running down her cheeks.

Our five hours of work and preparation were literally collapsing before our eyes. It was a catastrophe. A daughter's simple wishes for a good birthday crushed, a father stuck in the worst kind of night-before-Christmas-toy-assembly nightmare, and a mother too stressed out about her made-from-scratch birthday cake decorated with leftover Halloween candy to pay much attention. Just two weeks in, the wheels seemed to be coming off our little experiment.

It's worth noting that a flamingo piñata would be no big deal in some households. There are families out there who make flamingo piñatas that not only dry with time to spare, but are beautifully decorated with pink feathers and handcrafted beaks made from native plants. There are dads who are so skilled and excited about this kind of family project that they install a small motor so the flamingo can flap its wings as the children take a Louisville Slugger to it. There are moms who have never used a Betty Crocker cake mix and don't need to use leftover Halloween candy because they make their own candy from the honey they harvest from their own back-yard apiaries. If you haven't figured it out yet, we are not that family. There is no danger of *Martha Stewart Living* doing a feature story on our innovative homemade birthday parties. We're that *other* family, the one that lives on the edge of household sanity.

But something happened on our way to a disaster: we came up against a moment that would become a routine part of our year, a moment when we were forced to innovate and roll with the punches and adjust our expectations. We had always dreaded these moments—we had them long before we jumped into this experiment—and did our best to avoid them. But as the year progressed, we came to look forward to them as a push to get creative and improvise.

That was not my attitude on the morning of the birthday party however. I was still in that I-would-spew-profanity-right-now-if-not-for-the-presence-of-my-children stage. But I had no choice but to move forward. I popped the smaller balloon in the flamingo's head and it miraculously held its shape. I knocked on it and it responded with a solid clunk. During our construction process, we'd been less concerned with shoring up the head for the abuse of the party goers than we had been with the body. With fewer layers, it managed to dry more quickly.

I called out, "Noel, the head is okay. We'll put the candy in the head."

She slinked back into the room and gave the head a knock and said, "But what about the body? We can't just use the head."

I said optimistically, "I'll fill it with bunched up newspaper and no one will know the difference. They'll think we meant to do it this way."

I cut a large flap in the body and started stuffing. Sure enough, it regained its shape, a little rumpled and saggy, but not too bad. I taped up the flap and went to work on the head, chopping a big enough hole to dump in the leftover Halloween candy we weren't using to decorate the cake. That was all we had time to do before Noel's friends started arriving. With no pink feathers or triangle beak or eyes, it looked like a newsprint version of a *Monster's Inc.* character: long legs, stocky round body—with one big round eyeball protruding from the body—propped on the end of a long stem.

The party went surprisingly well. The cake was a hit and the homemade pottery bowls made for a fun project and party favor. When the time came for the piñata, I tied a rope around the neck of our forlorn flamingo and hung it from the banister. As the kids lined up to take their shot at the hanging effigy, they looked like some kind of juvenile ninja-training class. The blindfolded kids took their turns at smashing open the head. They were totally unfazed by the creature and went at it like any other piñata. The ridiculousness of it all created an infectious giggle in the room. After a couple times through the line, one of the bigger kids took a huge swipe that made a pure connection, and the head went flying across the room, leaving the long neck of the deceased bird holding up the limp body. With a big cheer, kids piled on the dismembered body part and grabbed the candy. I looked on at the gruesome scene with a kind of twisted pride, the first ever eight-year-old-birthday flamingo decapitation.

At this point in the year we were working with more of a fourfold motto than a fully formed moral compass for our lives as consumers. But what was quickly being unveiled was the hidden pattern of consumption that had been driving us all these years. We had been operating out of a sense of scarcity: scarcity of time and money, scarcity of energy and emotional availability. We woke up every morning feeling the burden of these scarce resources and were driven by this, shaped by this perpetual shortage, like there was some hidden embargo somewhere that mucked up the works.

In his book, *Divine Economy: Theology and the Market*, Stephen Long says that our basic forms of economic life are based on models of scarcity, that they actually demand it and create it. By contrast, he notes, the Christian God operates from the perspective of plenitude and abundance.[3] He asserts that the Christian story offers up an alternative way of living, drawing from the deep well of God's abundance. He writes, "God's inexhaustible plenitude suggests that we need not try to consume creation as our own. We need not cling to creaturely life, nor seek to flee from it. Instead, its desires can be properly ordered. This plenitude invites us to learn to participate in God's own perfections, in a simplicity of life that rejoices in cooperation and gift rather than in conquest, competition and acquisition."[4]

Simplicity is not the first word that comes to mind as I reflect on Noel's birthday party. It was complex and exhausting and complicated and inefficient. But it did arise from the "simplicity of life that rejoices in cooperation and gift" as opposed to the complexities of acquiring items across unfathomable supply chains. It was based on the simplicity of a household economy of time and skill and using what was at hand. And it did seem properly ordered, with parents and children elbow to elbow, splattering goo on each other, living in the wonder of uncharted shared experience. The other path was like a well-oiled machine that parents around the country had perfected in an effort to pump out a smooth birthday celebration. We were discovering the importance of proper complexity.

Later that evening, after we'd swept up the carnage from the day's events, I asked Noel how she liked her party. She spoke glowingly about the whole affair and without any prompting she exclaimed, "My favorite part was the piñata." I think she had in mind not just the joyous chaos of the flamingo head flying under the living room coffee table, but all the time we had spent preparing, the precarious moments of uncertainty that we had endured together, even the inconvenience of the whole thing. It had gathered us together. It caught us up in a different kind of family story where money and time are not oppressively in short supply, where she is not a cog in a family machine but, as Wendell Berry puts it, a child who belongs "to the world of love."

CHAPTER 4

Reading the Signs

A T FIRST WE TREATED OUR PLANS FOR THE YEAR AS A loosely held secret. This was especially true with our church. It's common for me to share about our family experiences in Sunday sermons to illustrate the message, but we were explicit from the very beginning that when it came to the details of our experiment there would be no sermon illustrations. The last thing we wanted to do was make a big public statement about our plans, only to sheepishly explain a few months into the year that we couldn't stick with them. It was also hard to explain our plans. The common response from friends when we outlined our plans was to ask, "You're doing what?" This was followed by a series of queries about specific items, punctuated by the question, "What are you going to do about toilet paper?"

In case you're wondering, we were able to locate a nearby paper manufacturer in Lewiston, Idaho, one hundred miles south of Spokane. They produce bath tissue, facial tissue, paper towels, and napkins, and they told us where we could buy their products in Spokane. Before we confirmed this supply of paper products, it was a fascinating exercise to imagine a world without rolls of soft white tissue. I did a little research and rumor has it that bathroom practices in America before the innovation of toilet paper included Sears catalogs, book pages, straw, hay, newsprint, and corncobs. Thankfully for the sake of our household, plumbing we didn't have to try out the corncobs.

After a while we got in the habit of telling people we were doing a year of local eating. People generally understood this and it didn't require too much explanation of the finer points of our rules. After we started a blog at the end of January, word spread and in late February we were approached by both *The Spokesman-Review* newspaper and *The Inlander* independent weekly to be interviewed about our experiment with a focus on local food—the topic du jour of 2008. Both articles, with large pictures of our smiling family, came out during the same week. The cat was out of the bag and we were officially stuck doing this for the rest of the year. There was no turning back now. It also became an open topic for discussion at church.

During the greeting time the Sunday after the articles came out, person after person said, "What you guys are doing, that's how we used to live." The farmers explained, "Back then all of our practices were sustainable and organic." Some of the older women told me about how they used to go on root cellar tours in the fall, admiring one another's bounty of canned goods and root crops. One of our outdoorsmen invited me to go hunting for turkey. "The season opens on Tuesday," he told me enthusiastically. I'd never been aware of opening day for turkey, nor have I ever fired a gun, but I took his offer seriously. It doesn't get much more local than that. Another church member pulled me aside and asked with a serious look and hushed tones, "What are you going to do about toilet paper?"

One particular comment from a parishioner grabbed my attention. As we stood outside church soaking up the early spring sun, I commented on all the snow on Mica Peak. He said, "You know, you used to see lantern lights up on Mica Peak at night." Curious, I asked for more information. He explained, "It was the moonshiners. In the 1920s people used to have their distilleries up there." I guess they call it moonshine because they did their work by the light of the moon.

The conversations were rich with history and local knowledge, and I was excited to now have the church as a partner on our journey. I still avoided talking about our experiences from the pulpit, but the question of how a life of faith intersects with issues of consumption was open for discussion.

HUGS AND STUFF

On the one hand, our year of plenty was three days in the making, a sudden spasm of creative folly. On the other hand it was years in the making, a journey marked with numerous signposts, some of them deeply rooted in our journey of faith as followers of Jesus. In November, just a month before embarking on our journey, we had a literal encounter with these signs, hints of where we sensed God leading us.

The day after Thanksgiving, just a few weeks before we would launch our plan for the new year, we took another trip to the western side of the state. We ventured into downtown Seattle to enjoy our regular ritual of going to Chinatown, dodging drug deals, and finding authentic Thai and Chinese food. We decided to do a little shopping before we ate so we hopped on the bus in the underground tunnel that runs like a vein through downtown and got off at Westlake Center, where the original Nordstrom store anchors the retail heart of the thriving city.

I grew up an hour from downtown Seattle. I have fond memories of huge salmon being tossed around at Pike Place Market and spending time on the waterfront eating Ivar's fish and chips and throwing french fries into the air like confetti for the seagulls. This city has shaped and formed me and yet as we rose from the depths on the escalators, I recognized that things had changed in the fifteen years I had been living elsewhere.

Seattle had gone from the B-list to the A-list of U.S. cities. The quaint hole-in-the-wall original REI store had moved from its accidental home off the beaten path on Capitol Hill to a silver-plated location, complete with a fifty-foot climbing wall and a view of the freeway. Microsoft had filled the neighborhoods around the city with a generation of millionaires. New-economy Amazon.com chose Seattle for its headquarters as old-economy Boeing left for Chicago. Even the working-class crab fishermen from Seattle were now stars of their own reality show on cable TV.

As we stepped into the pulsating crowd of shoppers, I was both energized and humbled, feeling a little like country folk coming into the big city with jaws agape at all the tall shiny buildings and fancy clothes.

At several intersections we noticed men holding well-worn placards that proclaimed, "Repent or Burn in Hell." If I recall correctly, the signs elaborated, "Many will say on judgment day Lord, Lord and He will say depart from me for I knew you not. . . . No liar, thief, backbiter, drunkard, fornicator, adulterer, murderer, or lukewarm churchgoer shall inherit the kingdom of God." That last one caught my attention because I knew it was their way of saying Presbyterians were on thin ice.

Whereas the crowds kept their distance from the street-corner preachers, a woman across the street was getting a joyous response with her handmade bold-lettered sign-on-a-stick that said, "Free Hugs." My instinct was to keep a safe distance from this woman and avoid eye contact, but Nancy couldn't resist. She leaped across the street and embraced the stranger with a big bear hug. So I followed her and ended up getting in a solid A-frame hug that I learned in the "appropriate personal contact" training class they give to pastors.

We looked around the sea of people and noticed there were about a dozen huggers spread up and down the block with the same "Free Hugs" signs, all of them with eager respondents waiting in line to get their hugs. I wondered if this was some new tactic of the Hare Krishnas or Scientologists. I found the ringleader of the free huggers and he explained that someone had posted a YouTube video and they were following his lead.

Juan Mann, the pioneer of the Free Hugs phenomenon, says it started as a spontaneous, personal response to feeling lonely in his hometown of Sydney, Australia. He explains,

> I got some cardboard and a marker and made a sign. I found the busiest pedestrian intersection in the city and held that sign aloft, with the words 'Free Hugs' on both sides. And for 15 minutes, people just stared right through me. The first person who stopped tapped me on the shoulder and told me how her dog had just died that morning. How that morning had been the one-year anniversary of her only daughter dying in a car accident. How what she needed now, when she felt most alone in the world, was a hug. I got down on one knee, we put our arms around each other and when we parted, she was smiling.[1]

He posted a video about his efforts giving free hugs, which went viral and has more than sixty million views to date. The popularity of the video led to a court case to allow free hugs in public places, an appearance on *Oprah*, and social-media-driven flash mobs in cities all over the world, including Seattle on the day after Thanksgiving.

We ventured down the street shoulder to shoulder with the crowd of shoppers and came upon yet another gaggle of sign holders, pumping placards with white letters on a black background that heralded a simple message, "Buy More Stuff." I was perplexed by these signs. Were they making fun of people who were compulsively buying more stuff, reflecting back to the crowd their wild-eyed zeal for more? Were they hired by the retailers desperate to pump up the appetite of the mob? I asked one of them what they were doing, and he said it was just for the fun of it. No agenda, just some postmodern splash on the surface of confused meanings.

These encounters with the signs stuck with me. We go through life guided by hidden slogans and symbols and it was refreshing to see these guiding narratives brought out into the open in the form of literal placards. This random, uncoordinated display in downtown Seattle actually captured some of the most compelling meaning makers in our lives. The "Free Hugs" signs pointed to the longing for connection and intimacy in relationships that preoccupies our days. The signs calling for repentance, while blunt, pointed to the hope for a relationship with God and despair at separation from God.

I was so struck by these signs I incorporated them into my sermon that Sunday, describing them as physical manifestations of the normally unseen signs we carry around. I spoke to our longing for God and our longing for intimacy. These themes are the bread and butter of the particular Christian tribe I call home, a free-hugs-meets-street-corner-preacher version of the faith.

But I wasn't quite sure what to do with the "Buy More Stuff" banners. Nothing makes a preacher happier than having three points to the sermon, so it seemed natural to say something about these others signs. Commerce is such a large part of our lives, a narrative that guides us in powerful ways, but I struggled to address its provocative message as we ramped up for the Christmas season of hyperconsumption.

The "Buy More Stuff" sign was utterly meaningless and overwhelmingly meaningful at the same time. While calls for repentance and hopes for intimacy resonated, the "Buy More Stuff" signs threatened to deconstruct it all, playfully taunting and confusing these other narratives as nothing more than detours on the eight-lane highway of buying as a way of life.

Even as our longing for reconciliation with God and others is twisted around in the midst of our compulsive urge to buy more stuff, I hadn't really been well equipped as a pastor or a Christian to navigate the minefield of consumption. If anything, my conversion to Christianity came booby-trapped with a disconnect between the inner and outer world, the life of spiritual seeker and materialistic shopper.

BUYING INTO FAITH

I became a Christian as part of a youth group, and while I didn't have much cause to reflect on the relationship between my faith and consumer culture in those early years, I can look back and see some ways that this relationship between my identity as a Christian and my identity as a consumer was being negotiated.

I remember the T-shirts from the Christian concerts and conferences I attended—almost all of them were knockoffs of the marketing slogan of the moment. "Got Milk?" became "Got Jesus?" The Burger King logo was transformed into a King of King's logo. "Life Goes Better with Coke" became "The After-Life Goes Better with Jesus." "Intel Inside" became "Jesus Inside," and so on. I never bought one of these T-shirts, but I can see how they started to shape my perspective on Jesus in a consumer culture. The implicit message in the fusion of slogans and logos is that Jesus is the supreme consumer product. The T-shirts are a recognition that the most powerful language structures and meaning-making words come from large corporations selling products. Instead of subverting the marketing mojo, the T-shirts implicitly communicate that the consumer life is fine, just don't forget that Jesus is better than a Whopper.

I don't want to make too much of these T-shirts. They are produced by people trying to make some money, not lay out complex theological positions about consumption. I guess that's part of the story, too.

Another formative experience for me in sorting through the relationship between faith and consumer culture was the little evangelistic booklet called *The Four Spiritual Laws*. It was created by Bill Bright and Campus Crusade for Christ as a tool to help people enter into a relationship with Jesus. The core message of the "laws" is "God loves you and offers a wonderful plan for your life,"[2] that in a world separated from God because of sin, God sent Jesus as a bridge and through faith in Jesus we have access to the God of wonderful plans. During my junior year of high school, my youth pastor led me through the booklet in his kitchen while he cooked up some corned beef hash on the stove. We flipped through the pages that culminated in a prayer of commitment to Jesus as Lord and Savior. After hovering around the fringes of faith communities my whole life, the grand scope of God's activity seemed to settle into the personal space of my life as I said that prayer.

In many ways I had already trusted in Jesus as my savior. I had been hearing about Jesus for years and I found him to be compelling. His rebellious love and radical servant life resonated with me deeply. Many times, in a variety of ways, I had put my weight down on the promises of Jesus. Mine had been a growing and evolving faith and walking through the laws that afternoon felt like an important step on the journey.

During my sophomore year of college, Bill Bright visited our Christian fellowship group. His presentation was a friendly dialogue with my college pastor. At one point my pastor asked him about the origins of the *Four Spiritual Laws* booklet that had been such an important part of my Christian experience.

Mr. Bright explained that he hired a marketing firm, giving them the assignment to take the message of the Bible and communicate that message in a simple and compelling way so people would come to faith in Christ. He explained how important it was that we use every means necessary to lead people to Christ. In an early '60s culture that was learning to flex its marketing muscle, it was important to turn to these resources and utilize them for the glory of God. So the same generation of marketing geniuses that brought us "Please Don't Squeeze the Charmin," and "Plop, Plop Fizz Fizz" penned the phrase, "God loves you and has a wonderful plan for your life," God's story as advertising copy. At the time it made sense to me that in a consumer culture Christians need to appeal to people as consumers. My understanding of God as a consumer product and people as spiritual consumers was beginning to take shape in more overt ways.

Over time, however, my initial comfort level with this seamless integration of the vision of following Christ and the vision of people as consumers began to crack. One particular experience during my season of preparing for pastoral ministry comes to mind.

I was hanging out at a coffee shop and got talking to another young man. As I was prone to do at the time I steered the conversation to God and Jesus and my conversation partner seemed to be really interested. For a good half hour I talked about faith in Jesus, quoting C. S. Lewis and Karl Barth. With every passing minute I grew more excited that I had a receptive audience and was sure my friend was inching closer to the kingdom. At the end of our talk I invited him to the evening service at church, and he accepted the invite. He was so enthused about our interaction that he reciprocated with an invitation of his own to a gathering he was having later in the week. I exchanged phone numbers with my prospective convert, excited about him coming to church that night and a bit curious about his gathering.

Later in the week I got a call from my new friend following up on his invitation. After some small talk, I asked for more details on who would be there and I probed him for information on the purpose of the meeting. While he didn't use the word multilevel marketing, it didn't take too much effort for me to figure out it was a recruiting meeting for pyramid foot soldiers. I realized that to him I was not a person so much as an object. I was a potential customer and client. More than that, I realized that his enthusiasm for the gospel of Jesus was predicated on the hope of luring me in. He would listen to my sales pitch if I listened to his. I explained that I really wasn't interested in being an "independent entrepreneur" and hung up the phone, feeling a bit exasperated.

In a flash of recognition I came to see our short-lived friendship for what it was: two sales people hoping to close the deal. Our relationship was completely contained within our shared vision of the other as consumer. While I was repulsed at the recognition of being objectified, my approach had been no more noble or humanizing. Under the veil of unconditional love and eternal concern, I had turned him into an object for manipulation. I was second-guessing my unquestioned acceptance of God as consumer product.

When I started life as an ordained pastor in a local congregation, I threw myself into the world of church shoppers and first impressions. I learned the metrics of marketing the church. For example, I was instructed by the gurus of church growth that people decide whether they are going to come back to a church during the first five minutes of their visit and that the sooner after worship visitors get a phone call from the church, the more likely they are to come back. I was living in a narrative world where God was the product and the church was the service sector of God's economy.

Thankfully it was a wonderful church full of real people, and the Spirit of God refused to be contained in my categories. While I unartfully imposed a vision of church as consumer culture, a story of Jesus' grace and mercy and love unfolded all around me, subverting my marketing schemes.

Still, the consumerism mentality is so tightly tied to the business of doing church that there were times I wondered if I should just make it official and get a job selling shoes. I had been in ministry for five years when we had a consultant come to our church to lead us through a strategic planning process. I was grateful and hoped he could help me figure out a more helpful vision for ministry.

After some preliminary discussions and mixer games, we came up against that point in strategic planning when you get to the hub of the matter. Our consultant prefaced this key moment by reflecting on his mentor, Peter Drucker, who upon his retirement had turned his attention from leadership in the for-profit world to focusing on nonprofits and even churches. The consultant explained that while Drucker's attention had shifted as he cast his attention to these different kinds of organizations, Drucker's essential question, which the consultant offered to us as our question, was the same: "Who is your customer?"

Apparently the most important question we could ask wasn't "Who is God?" or "What is the nature of the church?" or "What does the incarnation of Jesus look like in today's world?" or "How do we follow the example of the disciples and dwell among the people, proclaiming the kingdom of God at hand?" The guiding narrative wasn't redemption or peace or love, it was consumption. The vision of personhood wasn't based on a person as God's beloved child, but rather on a person as an autonomous chooser of goods and services. What had been subtle hints on T-shirts were now explicit and clear.

Had Peter Drucker's framing question landed in my lap during my first two years of pastoral ministry I would have launched myself even more intensely into melding faith and consumerism. But five years into the journey I hungered from the deepest places for a different narrative from which to do ministry.

GETTING THE STORY STRAIGHT

Around the same time, I had been reading through the book of Jeremiah and was struck by the core failure of God's people. Jeremiah judges that failure saying, "They did not ask, 'Where is the LORD, who brought us up out of Egypt and led us through the barren wilderness, through a land of deserts and ravines, a land of drought and utter darkness, a land where no one travels and no one lives?'" (Jer. 2:6).

The core failure is that they lost the story and lost sight of the God of the story. I felt that judgment in a personal way as I wrestled with the unsettling integration of consumerism and Christianity. I despaired that perhaps I had somehow lost the story.

Lesslie Newbigen gets to the core of the issue when he says, "The way we understand human life depends on what conception we have of the human story. What is the real story of which my life story is part?"[3] Alisdair McIntyre says the same thing in a different way: "I can only answer the question, 'What am I to do?' if I can answer the prior question, 'Of what story do I find myself a part?'"[4] Looking back at the subtle and not-so-subtle clues of my spiritual formation, I can see that even in the midst of the greatest story ever told—the "real story"—I was caught up in a way of thinking in which life was framed around a story of consumption and commodities, self-interest and meeting needs. We lifted up signs rooting for salvation and intimacy as the guiding narratives, but the "Buy More Stuff" signs were bigger and louder and, at the end of the day, the ones we trusted more.

I should note that I believe the message of the *Four Spiritual Laws* is true. I believe that Jesus is the bridge, the mediator, between humankind and God. I believe that God's will for my life is wonderful. I believe that I need to repent and commit my life to God, trusting in Jesus as Lord and Savior. But looking back I can see that while true, the "laws" as they were written up within the imaginative world of a marketing firm, get the story wrong. It's not the story of a God who comes to individuals offering wonderful things, it's the story of a God who comes to the world sacrificing his very self, and at the heart of the sacrifice is the promise of redemption and forgiveness, a kingdom coming on earth as it is in heaven, a gathering up of all things in Jesus. The story is to take up your cross and follow Jesus, come and die that you might live, cast aside all allegiances at all costs and trust in Christ as Lord.

I believe in evangelism and being prepared and equipped to tell people about the hope we have in Jesus. But it perverts the story of the church to envision people as projects to convert, or friendships to leverage. In a world prone to coerce and manipulate, the church should come offering free love, and even free hugs.

I also believe that a good church is attentive to meeting the needs of the people and shouldn't be shy in telling neighbors about what is available to them in the community of faith. I believe in direct mail, good Web sites, and advertising in the newspaper. But putting the question "Who is our customer?" at the heart of the church's mission gets the story completely wrong. The greatest gift the church has to offer its neighbors is to recognize them as something *other* than customers. In a world where everyone is constantly reduced to objects, the church ought to be a refreshingly humanizing force. The story of the church is to envision people as beloved children of God who are irreducible.

I've spent the years since that consultation framed around Peter Drucker's famous question looking for better questions and a better story to guide life in the church and my journey as a Christian. Our year-long venture was part of that search, actively subverting the consumer status quo in our personal lives, trying to figure out what to do with the "Buy More Stuff" sign even as we sorted through questions of salvation and intimacy.

Early in 2008 I reread a book called, *The Consuming Passion: Christianity & the Consumer Culture.* The book title was my first choice for the title of our blog, but Nancy thought it sounded too much like a dime-store romance novel.

I like what Rodney Clapp, the editor of the book, has to say in the introduction about a thoughtful way for Christians to respond to the influence of consumerism in the Christian community. He says:

All its elements are not simply good or bad. It is pervasive in both grossly obvious and infinitely subtle ways. It is profoundly rooted in faith, culture, and society as we now know them. To the degree it is toxic, it is an ivy in the garden with its tendrils wrapped around and through our most beautiful flowers and our most essential vegetables. It could not be violently or wholly extirpated without destroying much that we rightly prize and protect. But just like such a vining plant it has grown too abundant and thick, so that it is now choking the life out of precious flowers and indispensable vegetables. Christians and other people of faith are among those who must gird themselves for a long, intricate, and difficult pruning.[5]

I'm convinced that too often the faith community has been behind the curve in addressing the powerful influence of the "Buy More Stuff" banners that surround us. Instead of being pioneers, we have accommodated the rhythms of our consuming culture. Instead of innovating tenable alternatives, we have tried hard to find ways of making faith fit into the prevailing practices of consumption. As many of us in the faith community are just beginning the journey of awareness around these issues, other communities among us are well along in the journey of disentangling and pruning. I am learning that for me, this requires a posture of listening as well as speaking. I remember many classes in seminary on learning how to speak, but very few on learning to listen. Along with piñata crafting and thrift-store shopping, our experiment was teaching me about listening.

II: Spring

Though as a man I inherit great evils and the possibility of great loss and suffering, I know that my life is blessed and graced by the yearly flowering of the bluebells. How perfect they are! In their presence I am humble and joyful. If I were given all the learning and all the methods of my race I could not make one of them, or even imagine one. Solomon in all his glory was not arrayed like one of these. It is the privilege and the labor of the apprentice of creation to come with his imagination into the unimaginable, and with his speech into the unspeakable.[1]

—Wendell Berry

Consider the lilies of the field, how they grow; they neither toil nor spin, yet I tell you, even Solomon in all his glory was not clothed like one of these. But if God so clothes the grass of the field, which is alive today and tomorrow is thrown into the oven, will he not much more clothe you—you of little faith? Therefore do not worry, saying, "What will we eat?" or "What will we drink?" or "What will we wear?" For it is the Gentiles who strive for all these things; and indeed your heavenly Father knows that you need all these things. But strive first for the kingdom of God and his righteousness, and all these things will be given to you as well. So do not worry about tomorrow, for tomorrow will bring worries of its own. Today's trouble is enough for today.

—Matt. 6:28-34 (NRSV)

L IVING WITHIN THE CULINARY CONFINES OF WINTER root crops, I have never been so attentive to the slightest hints of spring as I was during those first months of 2008. It was a hard winter with record snow and biting cold. Spring was taking its sweet time to arrive, so in the middle of February with no sign of resurrection to be found, I took matters into my own hands. I ordered a used electric heater on eBay and put it in our small six-by-eight-foot greenhouse. I crunched my boots step-by-step through a foot of snow to fill the greenhouse with our first trays of seed starts.

In Spokane, the traditional last freeze date is May 15, and most seed packs offer instructions about starting seeds indoors a certain number of weeks before the last freeze date. Most seeds are best started six to eight weeks before this important date but I was unfazed. This year the best time to start seeds would be fourteen weeks before reaching the seasonal milestone.

I thought I could sneak around the limits of the seasons: length of days, soil temperatures, hard freezes, long shadows from a low-slung sun. I attended to these realities initially only in as much as I wanted to overcome them, to contort them to my timing. My creative energies went into how to get around them and get a leg up.

But I learned that year the lesson I learn every year, only harder. These boundaries can be stretched and fudged, but they cannot be overcome. They are boundaries beyond my control, marching forward at their own mysterious pace. Efforts to fool the seasons in a particular place always, yes always, end up making us the fool.

My hydroponic farmer friend, who grows food in the climate-controlled environment of a greenhouse twelve months a year, tells me that even he is bound to these seasonal boundaries. A tomato grown in August in a hydroponic greenhouse will taste just like a tomato grown outside in the soil, but in the middle of winter, when the sun is in short supply, all the lights in the world won't make that tomato taste like it is summer fresh. He says, "You can't fool the plants."

I put my starts in the soil well before the last freeze date and instead of growing in the warmth of my optimism they sat shivering in the near-freezing soil. They looked up at me in their hypothermic state and asked, "Why?" Plants don't grow just because they have water and soil. They grow in a complicated interaction of soil temperature, length of days, direct sunlight, and moisture. Without the proper mix of these factors the plants just sit, sometimes rotting or freezing, but never growing.

As the futility of my efforts to grow food set in, I began to take a different perspective. My view shifted and my attention turned to what the spring thaw offered up, instead of what it disallowed. With these new eyes to see I noticed the wonder of rhubarb bursting out of the ground, crinkled and leathery. Not far from my suffering plant starts were what gardeners call "volunteers." Here I had been forcing my will on plants like a garden tyrant conscripting a fearful population of early season vegetables when, from every corner of the yard, there were volunteers coming forward of their own free will—cilantro, dill, chives, and dandelions.

Yes, dandelions. They are a tasty source of fresh spring greens that I've proven I can grow year after year. This crop is a good confidence builder for any gardener nursing his wounds from a fickle spring.

In March, when I was on dinner duty, I wandered the property and gathered a bounty of the green serrated leaves and tossed them into an early spring salad that consisted of locally sprouted mung beans from Idaho, matchstick carrots from a nearby Greenbluff farm, and dandelion leaves from cracks in our driveway. The true test was to see how the girls responded to eating "weeds."

Noel said, "It kind of has a zing to it."

Lily commented, "It kind of makes you perky, but it's really good."

As we made the first transition from one season to the next, we were learning to pay keen attention to nature—and not just to scheme and contrive a way around it. We were learning to see gifts where there had once only been inconveniences. We were learning that life has certain immutable rhythms and that there is unexpected joy in letting creation lead the dance.

As Jesus puts it, consider the lilies, tune into the smallest details that point to the biggest truths: Creation, Creator, Created. It's probably no coincidence that Jesus chose among the earliest and most tender of spring wildflowers to highlight God's glorious grace. Lilies put on the most elaborate of displays, breaking the dull drone of winter gray and announcing the certainty of the turning of the seasons.

More broadly Jesus is saying consider the glorious springtime. Before you plant and harvest and "make" the world in the heat of summer, remember that the world was made, and you are caught up in the drama of the making.

To borrow Noel and Lily's words, this new attentiveness has a zing to it. It's uncomfortable and confining, but it's really good. It kind of makes you perky.

CHAPTER 5

This Commodified Life

The first thought may be a recognition of one's ignorance and vulnerability as a consumer in the total economy. As such a consumer, one does not know the history of the products that one uses. Where, exactly, did they come from? Who produced them? What toxins were used in their production? What were the human and ecological costs of producing them and then of disposing of them? One sees that such questions cannot be answered easily, and perhaps not at all. Though one is shopping amid an astonishing variety of products, one is denied certain significant choices. In such a state of economic ignorance it is not possible to choose products that were produced locally or with reasonable kindness toward people and toward nature. Nor is it possible for such consumers to influence production for the better. Consumers who feel a prompting toward land stewardship find that in this economy they can have no stewardly practice. To be a consumer in the total economy, one must agree to be totally ignorant, totally passive, and totally dependent on distant supplies and self-interested suppliers.[1]
—Wendell Berry

WHEN WE BEGAN OUR ADVENTURE, WE STILL HAD QUITE a bit of food in the cupboards and freezer. Slowly but surely our stockpiles started to dwindle. Staples we'd never even thought about suddenly became precious jewels of the kitchen. For the first time in our married life, we didn't have a minimum of five boxes of cereal in the pantry. We had none. By March we were sugar free or sugar deprived, depending on how you look at it. Instead, we ate a lot of honey from Tate's Honey Farm, located just a few blocks from our house, and experimented with palm sugar from Thailand. We used homemade butter instead of cooking oil. Bananas were a faint memory. We ran out of computer paper in mid-February and resorted to printing on the back of the kids' coloring pages. Paper towels and napkins were going fast.

One glimmer of abundance at the beginning of the year was an almost full, five-pound bag of Toll House chocolate chips. I viewed this bag as a little refuge of indulgence. I would grab a handful here and there throughout the week. It was such a huge bag that I chose to focus on the positive. I would say to myself, *I can't believe there are still so many chips left!* It was my little fantasy of the never ending bag of chocolate.

Then, one dire early spring day, Nancy burst my fantasy bubble when she discovered the nearly empty bag of chips.

I now know the shame and social alienation of the ancient villager who was caught raiding the winter supply of fruit wine. I rationalized my actions, saying, "We were going to run out soon anyway." Nancy, unimpressed with my logic, told me that as part of my penance I had to write about my transgressions on the blog. She also hid the few remaining morsels of chocolate and refused to tell me where they were.

On a side note, Thailand is probably the worst source of sweets and dessert foods in the world. Mung bean balls anyone? Or how about a red bean popsicle?

One by one it seemed like every standard food item in our kitchen went down in the flames of the cruel logic of commodities markets. Early on, we turned to the Internet to help us find locally sourced staples like sugar. It didn't take me long to find an article about a sugar beet processing facility only a couple hours to the west of us in Moses Lake. It turns out sugar is made from either sugar cane—which I honestly thought was the only source of sugar—or sugar beets. These beets bear little resemblance to the red beets for sale at the farmers' market. These dusky hunks of tough fiber are chemically processed to produce sweet white granules of sucrose.

I dug a little deeper, eager to find out where to get sugar from this company, only to learn that the plant was shuttered in 2002 due to a bad harvest of sugar beets in the region and mechanical problems at the plant. The closest source of sugar was Boise, Idaho, well out of the range we'd set for ourselves. Upon discovering this, I went to the cupboard and grabbed a handful of chocolate chips to console myself.

DAIRY SPIES

Dairy products are a big part of our diet, and we were eager to find out where we could buy local cheese and milk. Because the labels gave no indication of the source of the milk and the folks at the grocery store didn't know, we took the kids on a field trip to Inland Northwest Dairy, the local dairy processor. We wanted to make sure our milk was processed locally and that it came from cows from eastern Washington and northern Idaho.

As we approached the large, industrial-looking lot filled with semitrailers under the shadow of five-story towers of milk, we felt that ringing of the internal alarm system that tells you you're about to break the rules. Maybe it was the fifteen-foot high chain-link fence topped with barbed wire or the clear absence of a public entrance, but I had a strange feeling we might get arrested, or at least accosted by a security guard. The smell of social anxiety in the air was confirmed when the kids yelled, "Daddy! Don't go in there! We're going to get in trouble!" Since when did it become such a radically subversive thing to see where our milk comes from?

Despite the kids' panic and my own second thoughts, we crossed the threshold and drove slowly through the maze of delivery trucks, trying not to make eye contact as we scouted out the entrance under a towering Darigold sign. We parked the car and, holding hands in solidarity, walked through the glass doors and up the stairs. It was the first of many mysterious boundary crossings we would make between the food on our table at home and the facilities that process and package it.

As we reached the top of the steps, I was surprised to find a series of interpretive displays explaining the dairy business. They were all a little dusty and had a 1960s patina about them. I imagined a time when that great hall was bustling with students in horn-rimmed glasses and poodle skirts out on field trips to see where milk comes from. But as we stood in the strange silence, not another person in sight, I had a feeling it had been a long time since large groups had visited the dairy.

One side of the hall was wall-to-wall windows looking down at a busy stainless-steel highway of machinery filling gallon jugs and little plastic pouches with milk (apparently milk sometimes get packaged in baggies). The kids' anxiety was transformed to joy as they stuck their noses against the glass and took in the scene. Lily said, "Look! That's our milk from school."

I also saw the familiar label of the milk that inhabits our family fridge. But in a moment of confusion, I also saw about five other brands of milk packaging, all getting filled with the same exact product. Maybe that's one of the reasons tours are out of fashion. The appearance of choice in the grocery story for commodity items like milk is often just a choice between logos and color schemes on the packaging.

After a while we wandered down to the corporate office entrance and peeked in. We were greeted by one of the managers of the dairy. "Hi," I said. "Our family is planning to eat food from eastern Washington and northern Idaho for the year and we wanted to know where your milk comes from."

After making sure we weren't some kind of government agents, he said, "Well, all the milk comes in from local dairy farmers."

"What about sour cream, yogurt, butter, and cottage cheese? Do you make any of that here?" I asked.

"No, we don't process anything here except milk: whole milk, two percent, and nonfat. All the specialty dairy in grocery stores around here is produced on the west side of the state and shipped over. Looks like you're out of luck on that," he said.

With an air of desperation in my voice I asked, "How about cheese and ice cream?"

"No, I'm not aware of any local sources. Of course there is always the WSU Creamery," he responded. The Washington State University Creamery in Pullman, an hour's drive south of Spokane, is famous for its Cougar Gold cheese in round tins and Ferdinand's ice cream, all made as part of the student-run dairy operation on campus. The only problem is that the thirty-ounce containers of cheese cost $20, and Ferdinand's ice cream is sold only at the on-campus ice cream shop. Cheese was suddenly thrust into the luxury item category of our consumer lives and ice cream and butter moved into the homemade category. We figured we could live without cream cheese and sour cream.

We eventually made the trek to WSU's relatively small cheese making operation. While we were there, the manager told us about the large Darigold cheese making operation in Sunnyside, Washington. According to the president of Darigold, it is one of the largest and most efficient state-of-the-art cheese plants in the world.

Nancy went to work the next day trying to figure out how we could get our hands on some of this "local" cheese. The folks in Sunnyside were very helpful, but in what would become another recurring experience, we found that a food system built around maximizing efficiency and profit does not lend itself to identifying where the food originates. It turns out that Sunnyside churns out over 400,000 pounds of cheese every day but most of it, at least at the time of our quest, was shipped to far off places like Wisconsin. So if we wanted local Pacific Northwest cheese, we might have had better luck on one of those cheese tours of Wisconsin. Another option was for us to find a restaurant that bought Darigold's forty-pound blocks from Food Services of America and have them cut off a chunk for us. Or we could find some friends who wanted to go in on buying the forty-pound block and share it. I also considered the possibility buying several blocks of cheese and becoming the neighborhood cheesemonger. Ultimately we splurged on gourmet cheese from the WSU Creamery, which is probably why I didn't lose weight during the year.

In other random cheese news, we were told that cheese from one manufacturer in Oregon is shipped to Oakland, California, to be shredded and then shipped back north to be distributed.

I want to digress for a moment to point out that while finding local sources for food was a necessary priority, our kitchen was not the only place we felt the strain of our rules. One morning Nancy started the day by declaring, "We have a crisis." She went on to list all the things we were about to run out of or needed to replace. In response to Nancy's distress, I came up with a list of possible locally sourced or used replacements:

Tin foil—used plastic shopping bags
Saran wrap—used plastic shopping bags
Sandwich bags—used plastic shopping bags
Cooking spray—used and melted plastic shopping bags?

Noel's jeans that all had holes in them—used plastic shopping
  bags
Nancy's running shoes—old running shoes lined with used
  plastic shopping bags
Used plastic shopping bags (We'd been using green bags from
  the grocery story since the beginning of the year, so our
  seemingly never ending supply of plastic shopping bags was
  quickly running out as well.)

WHEAT IS WHEAT, OR IS IT?

A few days after our visit to the dairy, we took a trip to the local
ADM flour mill. It had a strangely familiar feel to it. Once again,
Nancy and I met with anxious protests from the kids as we pulled
up to the security guard at the entrance. We explained our intentions and he surprisingly let us proceed. (I think the general rule
when infiltrating local food processors is to always bring innocent
looking first- and third-grade girls with you.) This time we weren't
allowed to go into the facility, but we were greeted by a friendly
employee at the door. We asked him the source of the wheat used
to make the flour and he confirmed that it was all from our region.

We couldn't go into the facility, but as we chatted we could see
through the half-open door pallets piled high with bags of different
brands of flour, differentiated only by the logo. The employee told
us there is one high-end brand of "stone ground" flour that ships
flour from Spokane to Portland, so they can run the already ground
wheat through their stone grinders, just so they can advertise it as
stone ground.

These trips felt like opening the curtain on the old man pulling
at levers in *The Wizard of Oz*. The stories and images and names
that led us to believe we were empowered with meaningful choices
in the grocery store were often just illusions of choice. The marketplace of commodities had stripped all the stories and names and

connections to the land from the food and distilled it down to the least common denominator: money.

The man from ADM summed up the situation by saying: "Wheat is wheat. Flour is flour. It's all the same. When my wife asks me which brand to buy I always tell her to just get the cheapest one."

The bargain hunter in me felt a small victory in this knowledge, like we'd acquired some choice insider-trading scoop, but I wondered if it was true: that wheat is wheat and flour is flour and everything is the same. If that were the case then our efforts to make connections with the farmers who grew the wheat that made the flour that went into Nancy's new weekly ritual of baking bread was an unnecessary, irrelevant endeavor.

Having accomplished our mission, we turned to head home when our new friend from ADM stopped us and said, "You know there is one brand of flour in the stores that's different than the rest. We get wheat from the Shepherd's Grain wheat co-op and grind and process it separately from the rest."

"Why do they want it processed separately?" I asked.

He said, "I've heard they use something called no-till methods of farming. I guess it keeps the soil from eroding. They call it 'sustainable farming' whatever that is. I don't know what difference it makes."

When I met Fred Fleming, the cofounder of Shepherd's Grain, at a Food and Faith Forum he introduced himself by saying, "Hi, my name is Fred, and I'm a recovering conventional farmer."

I responded, "Hi, my name is Craig, and I'm a recovering conventional consumer." It was a match made in heaven.

Through my friendship with Fred and other farmers I've learned that in spite of what the ADM employee told us, there is a difference, that everything is not the same, that even something as basic and essential as wheat is not, as some would lead us to believe, a generic, story-less, land-less, people-less commodity.

Fred explained that there are different varieties of wheat that farmers grow on dryland in the Palouse region around Spokane: hard red winter wheat that's planted in the fall, and soft white wheat that's planted in the spring. I learned that different varieties of wheat have different nutritional content and different uses in the marketplace.

Most of all he helped me understand the different methods of planting wheat. Shepherd's Grain farmers use the no-till method. Instead of relying on conventional tilling methods with broad blades pulled behind the tractor that dig into and turn the soil, no-till farming uses "seed drills" that are pulled behind the tractor with minimal impact on the soil structure. Instead of digging up the previous season's stubble, the roots stay in the ground, helping the land retain water for next year's crops and, most importantly, preventing erosion.

My conversations with Fred led me to a book by David Montgomery called, *Dirt: The Erosion of Civilizations*. To my dismay, I learned that the "thin brown line" of top soil that covers the earth is more complex and more endangered than I could have ever imagined.

I had no idea that, according to the United States Department of Agriculture, it takes five hundred years to create an inch of topsoil through natural processes.

I never understood that in many tropical regions the rainfall eventually leaches all of the nutrients out of the soil itself. As Montgomery puts it, "Most of the nutrients in these areas reside not in the soil but in the plants themselves. Once the native vegetation disappears, so does the productive capacity of the soil. Often too few nutrients remain to support either crops or livestock within decades of deforestation."[2] The richness of the tropical rainforest is in the way it recycles the nutrients, not in the inherent richness of the soil. No wonder the tearing down of forests in the Amazon is such an important issue.

I was shocked to find out that farming in America leads to the erosion of millions of tons of soil every year, that when added up, it amounts to "enough soil to fill a pickup truck for every family in the country."[3]

I was especially intrigued to find Montgomery citing the results of a study done in the mid-'80s comparing two dryland wheat farms near my home in Spokane to illustrate the problem of soil erosion and farming methods. As he describes it, both farms were first plowed in 1908, one never using commercial fertilizers and the other using commercial fertilizers since 1948. Both farms boasted the same income, one leaving the field fallow every third year for a cover crop and the other harvesting continuously but paying big bucks for fertilizers and pesticides. That farm harvested more wheat but had much higher expenses that canceled out any economic advantage. Most importantly, the researchers found that the organic farm was actually building topsoil over time, while the conventional farm had shed six inches of topsoil between 1948 and 1985.

Montgomery sums up the study by saying, "With fifty more years of conventional farming, the region's topsoil will be gone. Harvests from the region are projected to drop by half once topsoil erosion leaves conventional farmers plowing the clayey subsoil."[4]

So I guess there is a difference. Commodities actually are connected to people and land and history. Wheat is not just wheat, and flour is not just flour, and when given a choice, it is actually possible for consumers to make meaningful choices beyond brand and image, choices that pay off for farmers, families, and the land.

Who knew a little trip to the local flour mill would put us in the middle of the grand drama of the rise and fall of civilization?

Farmer Fred has not only taught me a lot about farming and land use and sustainability. His perspective as a recovering conventional farmer has challenged me as I consider the task of integrating faith and the details of everyday life such as buying milk and flour. You could even say he's got me thinking about what a recovering conventional Christian might look like. In describing the efforts of Shepherd's Grain, Fred explained that, in response to issues like those described in Montgomery's book, they are seeking to understand the soil not just as a medium in which to grow wheat, but as an integrated part of the process of life. I am learning that what farmers like Fred are doing agriculturally, I need to do theologically and pastorally in the church. Like farmers, our lives have become disintegrated and fragmented by rapid cultural and technological change. Maybe we've imagined the whole world as little more than a medium for growing souls, pushing and pushing until we erode the fertile topsoil that's essential to our faith—justice, goodness, mercy, compassion. Imagine what might change if we thought of the earth and everything in it as part of God's redemptive plan, as an integrated process of life breaking out "on earth as it is in heaven." Maybe even our stop at the dairy aisle and our choice of flour could be fertile ground for faithfulness.

CHAPTER 6

The Kingdom of God Is Like
a Farmers' Market

ONE OF THE CATALYSTS FOR OUR YEAR OF PLENTY WAS the inaugural season of the Millwood Farmers' Market in our church parking lot. The idea for the market came from Kelly, a junior-high student in our congregation who lives just two blocks from the church. She hatched the idea on an aimless summer day in our sleepy historic mill town on the urban fringe of Spokane.

Millwood Presbyterian Church and the town of Millwood grew up in the 1930s around the Inland Empire Paper Mill that still chugs away next to the Spokane River that borders the town, spinning out massive rolls of newsprint and boldly blowing its horn to signal the change of work shifts. A while back, the mill stopped marking the hours with the loud blasts because they no longer manage the flow of workers coming and going with loud noises. But word on the street has it that the neighbors complained so much about the now missing marker of their days that the mill brought it back. So today, for miles around, the arrival of morning, midday, and afternoon are signaled by a classic factory whistle.

Our church also used to mark the days by broadcasting the beginning of worship on Sunday mornings with an organ prelude from its five-story bell tower. Ironically the neighbors complained so much about the noise that we stopped. No one can remember the exact circumstances or when it happened, but somewhere along the way the tower went silent.

These two sirens of community life, one silenced and the other passionately embraced, are descriptive of the cultural landscape not only in Millwood, but in communities across North America. There is a longing to be anchored in a place and a people and a story, but for many neighborhoods the church is no longer looked to as that place of orientation. While people grasp after echoes of now-meaningless signals of work shifts at the mill, they experience the clarion call of the church as noise and distraction.

Millwood is split in half by a busy set of railroad tracks, and the chugging engines are required to blow their blood-curdling, conversation-stopping sirens at the unprotected intersection right next to the church parking lot. The streets are lined by gnarled eighty-year-old Norwegian maples and the old storefronts of Main Street have become home to an eclectic mashup of locally owned businesses: a homey bakery, a Masonic temple, a yoga studio, a taxidermy shop, an espresso drive thru that doubles as a tanning salon, a tavern, and a book store/restaurant that boasts both a classic soda fountain and a talented resident artist who specializes in drawing celebrities from the fantasy/adventure genre of cinema. Beautifully detailed oil paintings of Kevin Costner from the movie *Waterworld* and Liam Neeson from *Star Wars: The Phantom Menace* supervise the lunch crowd from a makeshift art gallery.

While most people love the town, and some wait decades to buy a house in the neighborhood, I can see how an eighth grader would feel trapped in some kind of Pleasantville time warp.

Kelly complained to her parents, "There's nothing to do here! This is a boring place to live. Nothing ever happens."

Instead of rolling their eyes and dismissing the adolescent complaint, Kelly's parents challenged her to do something about it. "What are some events and activities we could have in Millwood that would make it more exciting?"

Kelly offered up several possibilities but settled on the idea of having a farmers' market with pop-up tents, live music, mingling crowds, heaping tables of fresh food, and the smell of lavender soap in the air.

Not Your Sausage's Grandmother

Less than a year later, after a whirlwind of serendipities too numerous to mention here, we held opening day of the Millwood Farmers' Market in the church parking lot with an eclectic band of thirteen vendors. A Mexican immigrant farmer brought in fresh asparagus from the Yakima Valley, known as the fruit basket of the nation. Tom and Louise, artisan bread makers, showed up with naturally fermented bread that was so fresh it steamed up the windows of their delivery truck. They unloaded the loaves from the back of the pickup like they were delivering a cord of wood, stacking them on the table while a line of customers waited for them to open for business. Students from the junior high school down the road brought tomato plants from their greenhouse and bragged to shoppers that their plants were "way better" than those for sale at Home Depot. Dave, a purveyor of grass-fed beef, lured customers to his booth with the smells of burgers and sausages sizzling on a grill and even sliced up samples for tasting. One man brought multihued green and brown eggs from his small farm homestead and laid them out on a card table while his young granddaughter manned the booth with a toothless smile. Duane, a seventy-year-old man who also sports a toothless smile, stacked up bottles of a healing concoction made from a secret American Indian recipe of birch bark and rubbing alcohol called, "That Stuff." He generously sprayed it on the elbows and knees of shoppers, proclaiming its healing powers. We even had a woman on acoustic guitar singing "Puff the Magic Dragon."

As I took in the scene of people wandering the booths, I wasn't quite sure what it meant for a church to run a farmers' market or, for that matter, for me as a pastor to help manage it. We had been in the process of sorting through the future of what was once a 1700-member congregation. The membership rolls had been in decline since the late '60s, and while our building inhabits the same city block as it did in 1927, there was a growing recognition that we were in a strange and different land. The normal equations of being and doing church were not adding up as they once had. Kelly's inspired idea seemed to mesh perfectly with our communal resolve to get the church out of the sanctuary and into the neighborhood. Our congregation had grown disconnected from our surroundings and was eager to reconnect.

Our congregation recognized this as a healthy change of pace, and yet opening day arrived without a well-formed theology or master strategy of farmers' market as mission. It was fun and exciting and adventurous but the connections with our faith were not altogether clear—that is until I overheard a conversation at the head of the line of people sampling Dave's sausages.

A woman, toothpick in hand and sausage in mouth, smiled at the beef rancher and said, "This is just like Costco," where samples of heated processed foods are available at every turn. Without hesitating Dave replied, "I can do something Costco can't do." Pointing to the sausage made from cows he raised in his backyard he said, "I can tell you the name of that cow's grandmother."

Dave not only knew which cow went into that particular sausage, he knew its family history. He pulled that cow from its mother's womb just as he had done for the mother. I'm aware that this may be more information than many of us want to ponder as we feast on spicy German sausage—maybe we'd prefer that our source of beef not have a name let alone a genealogy. But for me, in that moment, Dave was an accidental prophet, clarifying and solidifying the important connections between this little farmers' market and the bigger story of what God was leading us into as a family and a church.

In a culture where people are increasingly isolated, where consumer goods are completely removed from their source, where the aisles of community life are as wide and high as a Costco warehouse, Dave witnessed to an alternative story: a story where there is a farmer's face to go with the hamburger and a cow's grandmother to go with the sausage. He testified to something essential that is lost in the efficient and cheap commodities that dominate our consumer lives, a hidden cost that doesn't show up at the cash register—the lost human connection between those who provide food and those who consume it. I couldn't help but see in Dave's comments the bigger picture of a loss of community connections. Not only are shoppers disconnected from farmers, but neighbors are disconnected from neighbors. We not only don't know the names of the farmers and the cows, more often than not we don't know the names of the people next door.

With one little quip Dave managed to capture the unlikely energy and enthusiasm people have for shopping on dusty asphalt with pop-up tents in parking spaces. People long for connection to a neighborhood of familiar faces. We want to know names and places, and I suspect we want to be named and placed ourselves. And while the neighborhood had silenced the church steeple years ago, there was now a new sound coming from the church. It might have been '60s music, but it was a signal that the church was stepping into the deep longings of the community. In doing so, we had stumbled into hints of God's dreams for a connected and whole world, a world where God dwells with the people and is their God and they are God's people, and everyone has the dignity of a name, even the cows.

The Power of Necessary Things

There is a simmering hunger for "community" in American culture. And while that longing is almost universally expressed these days, the practice of community too often falls in a sentimental muddle. The words "community" and "authenticity" are lobbed into conversations like Duane's miracle cure-all for what ails us, but once the initial warm-fuzzy feeling wears off, from having said the words, we are not any better equipped for true experiences of community. We might fight for the local paper mill to keep its horn blowing, signaling bygone days when everybody knew their neighbors, but at the end of the day it's just nostalgic noise.

The challenge of forging authentic connections in community reminds me of the intense season as a pastor following the 9/11 terrorist attacks. There was this great awakening and renewed commitment to sharing life. As a pastor I experienced what every other pastor in American experienced—our churches began to fill up again. Everyone was talking about a great spiritual awakening throughout the country.

It took only three months for church attendance patterns to return to pre 9/11 levels. (The Barna Research Group issued a report titled, "Five Years Later: 9/11 Attacks Show No Lasting Influence on Americans' Faith.") If the heat and intensity of current political and cultural divides is any indication, church attendance patterns weren't the only things that very quickly returned to normal. The greatest cataclysm of a generation was not enough to shake us from business as usual, which is more independent, fast paced, and scattered than truly mutual connections demand. For some reason, most people were not able to translate the renewal that stirred deep inside them into authentic, enduring change. We thought things would never be the same again, but then they were and we are.

It begs the question: What does it take to break us out of our isolation and forge authentic connections in community? If an event with the transformative power of the 9/11 attacks failed to bring about lasting change in community connections, perhaps it's ridiculous to see an ordinary farmers' market as an answer to these longings. But I have come to believe that ordinary might be just what we need.

As of this writing we're wrapping up our fourth summer of hosting the Millwood Farmers' Market in the church parking lot. Dave's opening-day comments still inform our sense of mission at the market. We seek to be a place of connection in a fragmented world, and we believe this serves as a living witness to God's kingdom. It has been interesting to see through the years how the neighborhood has responded.

About halfway through that first season I was trying to explain to someone over the phone how to get to the church for worship and middirections they interrupted and said, "Oh, are you that building next to the farmers' market?" It's now standard practice around the church office when someone calls for directions to ask them if they know where the Millwood Farmers' Market is located. That's usually all that needs to be said to help people find the church.

I recently observed someone from the neighborhood giving an out of town visitor a tour of Millwood, pointing out the places of interest. When they got to the church parking lot she pointed to the bare asphalt and said, "We have a farmers' market here in the summer. It's awesome." Who would have ever thought our parking lot would become a point of pride in the neighborhood.

One response to the market was especially surprising. On a Wednesday during the market an elderly woman approached me. She said, "You're the pastor of the church aren't you?"

"Yes I am." I said.

"I really appreciate all the things your church does for the community. I come to the market every week when I can. I love the way it brings us together. In fact I'd really love to become a member of your church. There's one problem though."

"What's the problem?" I asked.

"Well, I'm an atheist. Would that be okay?"

Without hesitation I said, "We'd love to have you be a part of the church."

She said, "I just want to be part of a community and I sense that this is a place where I could belong. I wasn't sure what you'd think about the whole atheist thing. I promise I won't try to convert anyone." I welcomed her assurances, but I suspected she may be the one in danger of conversion. Our conversation seemed to indicate that there was indeed something powerful at work at this ordinary gathering of farmers, artisans, and neighbors. Meaningful connections were being made. Boundaries were being disrupted. In a small way, *community* was becoming more than just a sentimental word.

For our family, the market was a breakthrough in our efforts to lay down new roots and reconnect with our community. That first summer ushered us into a surprisingly satisfying weekly pilgrimage to the church parking lot. The girls played with other kids from the neighborhood, listened to music, ate dinner, pleaded for free honey sticks from Mr. Tate, the honey vendor, and pink frosted cookies from the Rocket Bakery. For the first time we were following the season's offerings, eagerly anticipating the arrival of green beans, then deep red cherries, then vine-ripened watermelon, and so on. The new arrivals were such a joy that we almost didn't notice the previous weeks' delights disappearing from the vendor tables. I found myself spending almost the whole afternoon hanging out in the parking lot chatting with the people I came to know as our Wednesday congregation.

When Nancy and I sat down in our puddle of discontent in December, the farmers' market was mentioned in passing. We were aware that it had an impact on us, but looking back now I can see that maybe it was the single greatest influence in shaping our plans for the year. We essentially asked on that night, "What if our whole life was like a farmers' market, where we know and care for the people who produce the things we consume?"

As our experiment began to take shape and our whole lives *did* start to resemble a farmers' market, there was a growing recognition that we had stumbled onto something that went well beyond the scope of our original intentions. Our intense focus on meeting our basic needs was opening us to the grand vistas of community and connection that had eluded us before. This was true with our neighbors who were transformed into joyful coconspirators in a black market of vanilla and chocolate chips, but it was especially true for our family relationships.

Our suburban kitchen became a production center for our farmers'-market lifestyle. I became the buttermonger. (I couldn't figure out how to make cheese, but I love the word *cheesemonger*, so buttermonger would have to do.) Using locally produced cream and a food processor, I made monthly butter deliveries to the family fridge. Nancy became the household baker, baking bread from scratch every Monday. The girls and I took on the challenge of making ice cream, with me attending to the technical details and them taste testing every batch, licking clean the whisk from the ice-cream machine.

Somehow the rhythm of doing ordinary things for each other was transformative. We were discovering what Wendell Berry says about the renewal of community life: "Community will start again when people begin to do necessary things for each other again."[1] Our rules were forcing us to take up crafts and skills, long ago deferred to others, in service to one another. They were a necessary part of our household economy. We joined with the farmers and artisans at the market, bound together in a network of everyday necessities.

RE-MONKING THE FAMILY

I realize that it's one thing to affirm necessary things as a path to forming meaningful family and community connections, but it's something different to propose that this is a spiritual path. It's one thing for a church to hold a farmers' market, but it's another thing to survey the scene unfolding in the parking lot and proclaim that the kingdom of God is at hand.

I find that, too often, we frame the formation of Christian community around the idea of escaping everyday life, as if it were the worst of distractions from things of God. It is assumed that God is hidden in the midst of daily necessities but is more available outside of these pressing rhythms. We are invited into the church sanctuary or retreat center to find God.

But what if we're mixed up in these assumptions? What if we've got it all wrong? What if, in fact, the most fruitful places of spiritual formation and connection with God and community are not in the removed, abstract places, but rather in the midst of the most mundane daily realities? What if God is among us at all times and all things, and the daily rhythms of life *are* the raw material of the spiritual life?

The monastic tradition certainly could be brought up as a counterpoint to this assertion. Some might say, "Surely there is a place for people to loose themselves of necessary things in order to attend to God, unfettered by the distractions of everyday life." Indeed, the monastic tradition looms large in the imagination of the evangelical circles in which I was reared. It is common for pragmatic-minded evangelical Protestants like myself to wax eloquent about the monastics while reflecting on the spiritual life. But too often this leads to a false idealization, an embrace of an idea of a spiritual life that stands in contrast to the lives we actually live out here, away from the abbey. And often it isn't even an accurate understanding of the monastic tradition. We grab ahold of the evocative traditions of monastic communities and take them captive to our false divides between the spiritual and material.

The best of the monastic traditions are not about separating and dividing up the spiritual from the necessary. Rather they are about wedding them together in a holy rhythm. I'm reminded of the story I once heard about a young monastic, who upon being told of his responsibilities on the small farm from which the community produced food, explained that he felt called instead to devote his whole day to prayer. He envisioned his days in the community unfettered by the urgency of creeping weeds and the burden of harvesting. His master, seeing his sincere intentions agreed to let him spend the whole day praying.

When the call went out in the evening for everyone to gather for dinner, the young monastic, famished from a day of rigorous contemplation of the divine, headed down the hall to dinner, only to be stopped by his master. The elder monk explained that just as he didn't wish for the young man to be distracted by farming, he didn't want him to be distracted by eating, and that just as he was free to forgo working in the fields he would also be allowed to skip the meals as well. He was instructed to head back to his room to attend to more important matters, while the others deal with crude and necessary things like chewing and swallowing.

I think, too, of the story of St. Teresa of Avila as reported by Eugene Peterson in his book, *Wisdom of Each Other: A Conversation between Spiritual Friends*. He describes a conversation between St. Teresa of Avila and the devil. He writes, "The Spanish saint was in the outhouse one day, reading her prayers and eating a muffin. The devil appeared and scolded her: 'How unspiritual! How abominably sacrilegious!' Teresa shot back 'The prayer is for God, the muffin is for me, and the rest is for you!'"[2] While Peterson highlights her humor, I am drawn to her practice of faith, so seamlessly integrated that not even the outhouse is beyond the reach of God's work in her life.

These anecdotes are by no means a comprehensive survey of the monastic tradition, but they do meddle with the idealized visions of people who dedicate their lives to prayer and the spiritual quest. Those who set aside a "normal" life to live dedicated to God are by no means freed from necessary things. If anything they are more intensely engaged by the daily rhythms of faithfulness and attentiveness.

I like the way author Denise Roy translates the depth of the monastic tradition into the realities of her modern life. She describes how, while on a spiritual retreat at a monastery, she came to understand her calling. She writes, "I had a revelation. My monastery is not a silent cell out in the wilderness. My monastery is a minivan. It is also a kitchen, a child's bedroom, and office. My monastery is in the heart of the world—in family life, with a child on my lap, in my partner's arms."[3]

Even more to the point, what if this focus on ordinary necessary things is the story we discover in the Bible? A story not of people escaping life to see God, but rather God meeting people in the midst of daily necessities and forming them as a people by anchoring them in these mundane realities?

The pattern in the Bible of forming community is surprisingly down to earth. There is a grand scope to the story of the Bible. The covenant with Abraham in Genesis 11 calls together a community that will be a blessing to all people in the world. It doesn't get more comprehensive than that. But when you get into the story and follow the community as it is shaped, the formative moments are almost always around the people of God sorting out how to do necessary things for each other, especially when it comes to food.

The first words out of God's mouth to Adam and Eve are, "You are free to eat." Not far behind is the warning, "You must not eat."

After their disobedience, God proclaims judgment, "Cursed is the ground because of you; through painful toil you will eat of it all the days of your life. It will produce thorns and thistles for you, and you will eat the plants of the field. By the sweat of your brow you will eat your food until you return to the ground, since from it you were taken; for dust you are and to dust you will return" (Gen. 3:17-19).

I can't help but see this curse of growing food from the ground being as much about formation as it is about judgment. Our humanity is tied up with the land, the food that it produces, and the toil of managing it. And the land would play a central role in the formation of God's people throughout the Bible.

In the wilderness it was the manna, gathered daily in the dew of morning that forged the faith of Israel. Once the people were settled in the land, the warning loomed large from Joshua to serve the Lord alone and remember that God "gave you a land on which you did not toil and cities you did not build; and you live in them and eat from vineyards and olive groves that you did not plant" (Josh. 24:13). Joshua was telling them to nurture a deep connection between the harvest of the vineyard and the God who made them a people and gave them the land.

To a people disoriented by exile in Babylon, Jeremiah said, "Build houses and settle down; plant gardens and eat what they produce" (Jer. 29:5). In other words, they were to attend to necessary things and do necessary things for one another. In doing so, they would find their way to God.

This pattern continued with Jesus as he sent the disciples out among the people to proclaim the kingdom of God. He told them to enter the homes of the cities to which they were sent. "Stay there," he said, "eating and drinking whatever they give you, for workers deserve their wages. Do not move around from house to house. When you enter a town and are welcomed, eat what is set before you" (Luke 10:7-8). The disciples had this grand vision of the kingdom of God to proclaim and live into, but the proclamation was always in the context of shared meals, working side by side with others, doing necessary things.

According to Luke, the early church exhibited these same characteristics. He writes, "All the believers were together and had everything in common. They sold property and possessions to give to anyone who had a need. Every day they continued to meet together in the temple courts. They broke bread in their homes and ate together with glad and sincere hearts, praising God and enjoying the favor of all the people" (Acts 2:44-47).

Scholars have hinted that this description by Luke may be a bit idealistic and unrealistic, and it certainly lends itself to utopian visions. But if we get past the sweeping generalities of the description, it's very down to earth and simple. They shared life together. They did necessary things, like bake bread and open the doors to their homes and share their lawn mowers. Okay, that might be extrapolating a bit, but I think the point holds.

James summed it all up when he wrote, "What good is it, my brothers and sisters, if people claim to have faith but have no deeds? Can such faith save them? Suppose a brother or sister is without clothes and daily food. If one of you says to them, 'Go in peace; keep warm and well fed,' but does nothing about their physical needs, what good is it? In the same way, faith by itself, if it is not accompanied by action, is dead" (Jas. 2:14-17).

In other words, faith that doesn't touch everyday life is dead. The community that is formed in such a way that doing necessary things for each other is not essential isn't much of a community after all. It is no more than spiritual sentimentalism or holy cliché.

As a family we had stumbled into unexpectedly holy rhythms of attending to everyday life. Our daily rituals and chores were transformed into a different kind of spiritual formation. We had a sense of experiencing aspects of the kingdom of God and to our surprise it looked like a farmers' market. *Community* was starting again in the Goodwin house and necessary things were leading the way.

CHAPTER 7

Bringing Down the World Economy

Love the quick profit, the annual raise,
vacation with pay. Want more
of everything ready-made. Be afraid
to know your neighbors and to die.
And you will have a window in your head.
Not even your future will be a mystery
any more. Your mind will be punched in a card
and shut away in a little drawer.
When they want you to buy something
they will call you. When they want you
to die for profit they will let you know.
So, friends, every day do something
that won't compute. Love the Lord.
Love the world. Work for nothing.
Take all that you have and be poor.
Love someone who does not deserve it.
Denounce the government and embrace
the flag. Hope to live in that free
republic for which it stands.
Give your approval to all you cannot
understand . . .

*. . . As soon as the generals and the politicos
can predict the motions of your mind,
lose it. Leave it as a sign
to mark the false trail, the way
you didn't go. Be like the fox
who makes more tracks than necessary,
some in the wrong direction.
Practice resurrection.*[1]
—Wendell Berry

*Askesis is to spirituality what a training regimen is to an ath-
lete. It is not the thing itself, but the means to maturity and
excellence. . . . It is the equivalent to the old artistic idea that
talent grows by its very confinement, that the genie's strength
comes from the confinement in the bottle.*[2]
—Eugene Peterson

WHEN WE FIRST PRESENTED OUR PLAN TO MY DAD, THE businessman, he summed up our scheme by saying in jest, "So, you're plan is to bring down the whole world economy." Little did we know that within a few months, talk of bringing down the world economy would be no joking matter. Our year of plenty was by coincidence also the year of the global financial collapse.

Early in the year I wrote a blog post highlighting my dad's comment pointing out that our intent was not quite so radical. For example, instead of buying Lily the $7 shiny new Beanie Baby at Toys-R-Us, we were going to buy the $2, not-so-new variety at Value Village. Somehow I didn't think the politicos and the architects of the global economy were shaking in their boots. The title of my blog post was, "Bringing Down the World Economy One Beanie Baby at a Time."

Much to my amusement, a few months later this blog entry showed up on Google as the number one search result of 1.3 million Web listings for the query; "bringing down the world economy." I only know this because there was suddenly a flood of inbound links to the blog from people searching Google for the roots of the economic collapse. I had fantasies of James Bond-like evil tyrants investigating ways to sabotage the world economy, only to discover that the key to bringing civilization to its knees was Beanie Babies. I also worried a little about ending up on some government watch list or being brought into election-year debates alongside Joe the Plumber. I'd be Craig the Butter Maker, the guy who single handedly brought the economy to its knees.

Our humorous stint atop Google was short lived, but the economic uncertainty of 2008 was serious business and it complicated our quest to define "plenty" in our lives. It begged the question; Can a year of economic collapse be a "year of plenty"?

We typically describe "plenty" in terms of money and net worth. This was evidenced by the Chinese zodiac prediction for 2008, the Year of the Rat. The forecast in January was optimistic: "The Rat year is a year of plenty, bringing opportunity and good prospects. It will be marked by speculation and fluctuations in the prices of commodities and the stock market; the world economy in general will boom. Business will be on the upswing, fortunes can be made and it will be an easy time to accumulate wealth."[3] I think I smell a rat or at least the worst prediction ever. It nailed the fluctuation part though and the economy did go "boom."

At the beginning of the year we had our suspicions that the financial definition of *plenty* was overrated, and if anything the economic peril of 2008 emboldened us to consider other ways of defining "plenty" and "enough."

I wish I could claim some grand scheme to take on the big corporations and tackle the ills of the global marketplace, but our plans mostly grew out of discontent with the patterns of consumption in the small space of our lives. If it was a protest, it was a protest against the numbing effects of the nonstop pursuit of the new and the next thing that would supposedly satisfy. It was akin to that feeling you have after five days on a cruise ship—overstimulated by decadence, wrung dry of every penny they could get out of you, and left wondering on the ride home why you're not more satisfied.

But this awareness was not leading us to seek the destruction of something, despite what my dad said. You won't find us vandalizing street-of-dreams homes or squirting glue in the locks of the local Starbucks. The world's economy seems to be doing a fine job of showing its weaknesses without our help. Maybe the truly radical thing to do in our culture of consumption is not to destroy something, but rather to create new and different ways of consuming.

PLENTY OF CHOICES

It's hard to say how we would have experienced the economic cliff dive had we not been preoccupied with finding a local source of toilet paper, but in the midst of our rules we experienced a strange sense of freedom in our financial lives.

Nancy stumbled onto the newly liberated experience of walking into a store with a very limited repertoire of purchasing possibilities. She noticed that the previously deafening roar of products competing for her attention was now a quiet chatter of just a few local offerings. It also helped that we now understood that all five brands of milk and flour have the same stuff inside the package. For the first time in my life I walked into a Costco and didn't pause in front of the gauntlet of big flat-screen TV's, entertaining the faint possibility that I could buy one of them. I did check once or twice for brands made in Thailand, but you get my point.

Our constraints gave us a new appreciation for the little things. For Nancy's birthday, I decided to surprise her with a bag of regular sugar. After all that she put up with as the primary baker/chef in the house, I figured she deserved some momentary sanity in meal planning and preparation. You can only so do much with palm sugar from Thailand.

I was thinking a one-pound pick-me-up would do, and for this purchase I wasn't too concerned about where it came from. This was an off-the-grid transaction, a small indulgence to help see us through to the end of the year, a mental-health necessity. But as I rounded the corner of the aisle at the local grocery warehouse, I was shocked to see a fifty-pound bag of sugar with the bold letters, "BOISE, IDAHO," emblazoned on the side. Boise was outside our range but it was close enough to make this purchase a no-brainer.

What happened next is a bit fuzzy. It could have been the onset of a new form of diabetic coma induced by being in the presence of large quantities of sugar after being deprived of it for long periods. To the best of my memory, I grabbed/hugged the pillowy bag of baker's special, went through the check-out line and slunk back to the car, looking left and right like I'd just pulled off a drug deal. All I remember for sure is pulling into our driveway with a fifty-pound bag of sugar in the passenger seat.

The challenge then became figuring out what to do with fifty pounds of sugar. I made sure to let the neighbors know that if they needed a little baggy or two, I was dealin'.

TRADE IN OR TRADE UP?

Part of the freedom we experienced was from dislodging the tenacious tentacles of stuff that grabbed at us, but the other side of it was the freedom to embrace things that were important to us without allowing the price to scare us away from our priorities. It was both freedom *from* and freedom *to*.

We'd been shaped in our consumer lives to pay attention to the price tag above all else. The meaning of products had been reduced to one simple metric with a hundred names: dollars, cents, rebates, coupons, two-for-one, three-for-two, no money down, six months no interest, closeout, clearance, going out of business, low, high, preferred card, members only, reduced, rolled back, and rolled out. There were other considerations, but they all paled in comparison to the almighty dollar. But now our focus on the source of products dethroned King Price from his tyrannical reign in our lives. We were learning different metrics that weren't metrics at all. We were learning stories that accompanied places and people and things. We were learning a new narrative in our household economy where incredible constraints invited us into some surprising freedoms.

Along with giving us a new appreciation for the little things, our purchasing constraints also gave us some surprising new perspectives on big things. A few days before Christmas 2007, Nancy accidentally crashed our minivan into a thousand-pound landscape boulder while trying to navigate a steep icy road near our house. Thankfully everyone was fine, but the car lost the showdown with the rock and when we returned from our Christmas in Seattle we got the verdict from the dealer: Old Bessie was mortally wounded, and they would have to put her down. So we limped along in our ten-year-old Subaru Forester while we awaited the insurance check.

We speculated that maybe we could get by with one car. Perhaps that could be our compromise for not driving a car that runs on french-fry oil, which seemed like the only way to strictly follow our rules. I looked into the possibility of rigging up an old Mercedes to run on used cooking grease, but, at least in this instance, it seemed a bridge too far. We discovered that a key to having rules to live by is not just sorting out how to enforce them, but also discerning when it's okay to break them. Following rules is always an improvisational act, a living compromise where the constraints of human life crash up against hopes and ideals.

When the check arrived, our conversations about living with one car converged with our ongoing speculations about making a family trip to Thailand. The same day we opened the envelope from the insurance company with a check for $4,000, I was online looking at prices for four tickets to Thailand leaving on Christmas Day 2008 for a two-week stay. They were, to our surprise, right around $4,000. Most of the surprise was how much it would cost to transport the family to Thailand and how little our minivan was worth, but we were also intrigued by the symmetry of a straight-up trade.

We were juggling a whole series of considerations that two months earlier would have seemed preposterous. Living with one car in an auto-dependant suburb with two elementary-age kids in soccer (with dad as coach), school, and piano lessons seemed unwise if not impossible. Even if we reconciled living with one car, any speculation about Thailand flew in the face of what had been our reasonable conceptions of what we considered responsible ways to use that large an amount of money. Maybe we should save it, or invest it for the long term, or put it towards the kids' college funds, or pay down the mortgage, or give it to charity—these all seemed like the decisions smart people would make.

However, in the early months of 2008, "smart" started to look a little different. I had always heard that if you have a ten-year horizon, the stock market beats any other investment, but 2008 would find the Dow Jones Industrial Average plunging lower than its 1998 value. We would have done better with our money under the mattress. Conventional economic wisdom seemed to be unraveling before our very eyes. Thankfully, a new wisdom was emerging for us.

The thought of spending a small fortune on a family "vacation" cut against the grain of our dollar-centric decision-making tree.

A few months earlier we would have recited a well-worn defense mechanism against disrupting business as usual: "Someday we'll do that, but right now we just can't afford it." In a world of infinite possibilities for how to spend our money and resources, we had mostly lived confined by the small, crowded ghetto of those possibilities.

After weeks of theoretical conversations about trading our minivan for a trip to Thailand, one afternoon I sat down in front of the computer and said to Nancy, "Today's the day. We're going to buy these tickets to Thailand."

"Really? Are you sure? That's so exciting!" Nancy spent her time in Thailand teaching English and coordinating teaching opportunities for young adults from the United States. She has dear friends there and had hoped we would someday make the trip, but her hopes were shielded behind a veil of reasonable options. As this far-off possibility became an imminent decision, she was overwhelmed with joy. The kids heard the ruckus and gathered around the computer as I entered the dates for our trip onto the airline's Web site.

"What are you doing, Dad?"

"I'm buying tickets to Thailand. We're going to leave on Christmas Day."

"We're going to Thailand? Really?!"

I took a break from entering our credit card information into the computer, clicked over to YouTube, and did a search for Thailand to show the kids some snippets of Thai life. We found a shaky video of a couple riding on huge elephants through a jungle and into a river.

"Yeah, we're going to go to Thailand, and we're going to ride elephants," I said as their eyes widened with disbelief.

We scanned through video after video of this far-off exotic place and with each image embraced more of the possibility that we would be in that place together. After we were sufficiently psyched up I navigated back to the ticketing Web site and finished entering the data. I reached the final screen, where it says in bold letters, "These tickets are nonrefundable," and gulped.

"Okay, I'm going to push the button," and with one twitch of my index finger we traded our minivan for an elephant ride in Thailand.

We were all a bit giddy the rest of the night. Nancy taught us some basic Thai phrases, and when it came time for bed we said good night to Noel and Lily, "sawatdee don yen" which means "good night."

Walking out of Noel's room, Nancy said, "I feel like we're back in college or something."

That could either mean we were being irresponsible and immature, or passionate and idealistic. It remained to be seen which would prove to be true.

THE HAPPINESS SPIKE

Our joy over the impending trip fit right in with what was starting to become a recognized fact—that experiences lead to more enduring happiness than material goods and possessions. A study by psychologists at Cornell University funded by the National Science Foundation found that when we get new cars, computers, and (add your currently most-lusted-after material object here) our happiness has an initial spike but we quickly adapt and integrate the new stuff into our lives. What was once extraordinary and fantastic and the best thing to ever happen to us becomes mundane, normal, and not half as cool as what our neighbor just brought home in a big cardboard box. After the new smell dissipates and the novelty wears off we move on to the next new thing, convinced that unlike all the other purchases, the consumer dream in the on-deck circle is the grand slam we've been waiting for.

The marketing industry has taken this basic truth of human behavior and turned it into a business model we are all familiar with. Victor Lebow, an economist and retail analyst, described this way of doing business in a 1955 article, just as the post-WWII economy was kicking into high gear:

> Our enormously productive economy demands that we make consumption our way of life, that we convert the buying and use of goods into rituals, that we seek our spiritual satisfactions, our ego satisfactions, in consumption. The measure of social status, of social acceptance, of prestige, is now to be found in our consumptive patterns. The very meaning and significance of our lives today is expressed in consumptive terms. . . . We need things consumed, burned up, worn out, replaced, and discarded at an ever-increasing pace. We need to have people eat, drink, dress, ride, live, with ever more complicated and, therefore, constantly more expensive consumption.[4]

While the consumption of stuff has become a way of life, the Cornell researchers tell us that at the end of the day our stuff doesn't provide us with happiness that lasts. When we seek our "meaning and significance" in consumer goods, we are the ones burned up and worn out. It is experiences that provide us with a more enduring satisfaction. Unlike stuff that degrades and depreciates over time, our experiences become a web of memories and meaning that get better with age. Like a good wine, these recollections mature and are refined over time, getting more complex and satisfying.[5]

Our decision to go to Thailand and invest in a grand shared experience was, for us, a dramatic example of how "plenty" was being redefined. In big and small ways the currency of our household kingdom was transitioning to an economy of plentiful experiences. We were learning what the Cornell researchers are saying, that an abundant life is not best measured by an accumulation of things, but rather by an accumulation of shared experiences. I'll share later about our experience in Thailand, but I can say here that we have never had a more plentiful and overflowing sense of abundance than we had during those weeks in east Asia. And it is true that the experience, instead of depreciating, continues to grow and gain value in our life together.

Thailand was unusual in our lessons about choosing experiences instead of stuff because it was financially costly. Throughout the year it was more common that our financial limitations or constraints were the avenue toward enriching experiences. In other words, not only were they cheap but they were like hidden treasures waiting to be revealed by financial constraints. For example, our Thailand adventure was more than a monetary trade-in. It meant we would spend the year with one car, which for us was an epic constraint.

And I want to be very clear about this: we know full well that living with one car is not much of an accomplishment. We have friends with kids who have lived with one car for years and it's no big deal. We have friends who live with no cars and bike everywhere. The only remarkable thing about our year with one car is that it was utterly impossible for us to imagine doing it before we actually did it.

And it's probably also important that I fess up that living with one car was by far the most frustrating, difficult, curse-inducing part of the year.

In April of 2008, our 1998 Subaru Forester with one hundred fifty thousand miles on it started overheating randomly and maliciously. The mysterious breakdown we had in Seattle on the night we came up with this plan blossomed into a full-blown leak in the head gasket. My mechanic called me up with the bad news: the whole engine would have to be taken apart and put back together. Two weeks later the car mysteriously broke down on the side of the freeway. Having just spent a bundle on the head gasket, I was anxious to hear about the cause of the latest breakdown, especially considering that this car was our only source of transportation.

My mechanics through the years have filled me with dread and fear of the timing belt breaking. They have explained in gory detail that if the timing belt breaks in a car's engine, the cams and valves will crash into each other, essentially ruining the whole engine. After having the car towed and dropped off at Rob's Auto, I got the call that I had been dreading my whole auto-owning life. No, the timing belt didn't break. I actually had it replaced when we had the head gasket fixed. Instead, the pulley that holds the timing belt had sheared off, meaning it was as if the timing belt broke, leaving the cams and valves all gouged and grooved. The whole engine would have to be rebuilt, and it would take two weeks to get it fixed. (A little friendly advice, when you have the timing belt replaced, go ahead and replace the pulleys, too.)

We borrowed a car from a friend for the two weeks our car was in the shop, and I have to admit that when we got the Subaru back, we were slow to return the loaner car. We had a glorious week of independence and freedom to roam at will. I didn't have to ride my bike to church at 5 a.m. on Sunday mornings to get ready for worship. Nancy and I didn't have to orchestrate our lives with the detail of a NASA mission, plotting out every minute of the day to make sure everyone's transportation needs could be accommodated. At the end of this week Nancy pleaded with me, "We've got to give the car back. I'm getting too used to having two cars." She sounded like an addict coming to grips with the reality that if she didn't turn back then, she'd lose the will to say no.

As was true for so many of our limiting experiences, they were difficult and inconvenient, but we found that they also opened us up to new possibilities. More often than not, these moments had gifts of plenty to offer on the other side of inconvenience.

For example, our life with one car forced us into a new tradition of walking the kids to school. One morning Nancy wasn't able to drive Noel and Lily to school and we had missed the bus. In a spontaneous, imaginative leap, I offered to walk the girls to school instead of heading off to work on my bike. I would drop them off and keep on trekking to the church on foot. We'd heard about a secret trail at the end of our cul-de-sac, and sure enough, with the clock ticking and the prospect of being late to class looming, we ventured down the street and confirmed the legend of the trail. We followed the route through a neighborhood and along a wooded path that dropped us off right on the doorstep of Pasadena Park Elementary. We never would have imagined walking to school if it hadn't been for our automobile escapades.

The girls and I were so excited by our transportation epiphany that we gathered the next morning on the porch to do it again, and this time Nancy decided to join us. Just as the four of us headed down the cul-de-sac to our secret trail, a third-grade neighbor came running around the corner after having missed the bus and decided to tag along. When we passed by another neighbor's house, two other children asked if they could join us. It was like Frodo Baggins from *The Lord of the Rings* and his band of fellow travelers. Our cadre of seven adventurers made the trek to school that day and, weather permitting, most days after that.

For a moment each morning, our lives felt a little like Huck Finn and Tom Sawyer pioneering new trails through the forest, tiptoeing around random barbed wire, passing mysterious teepees cobbled together with fallen baby Ponderosa pine trees, marveling at a neighbor's garden bursting with dahlia flowers, petting every dog along the way. Every morning brought its own adventure. One day we had to take a wounded adventurer to the school nurse because of a fall. On another outing we accidentally walked through a private estate in the middle of the woods. We waved sheepishly to the stranger sitting down at his breakfast table as our walking school bus wandered down his well-groomed driveway. Another day we found a deer skull. Who knew what each day would bring? Maybe a cave or a treasure map would be next.

A Kick in the Askesis

Our experiment was disrupting the status quo, freeing us up to embrace experiences instead of stuff. We were learning the counter-intuitive lesson that with meaningful constraints comes freedom, freedom from possessions that fragment our lives and freedom to embrace what we truly value. We were learning about something that the Christian tradition calls *askesis*.

It's common to fantasize that the pathway to fulfillment comes from unbounded freedom, but the wisdom of the ages is that it's actually in wrestling with limitations that we grow. Askesis is an intentional exercise of entering into limitations with a goal of growth and maturity. It is the Greek root of the word *asceticism*. I like the way Eugene Peterson describes askesis in his book *Under the Unpredictable Plant: An Exploration in Vocational Holiness*. He writes:

> We are familiar with the frequently beneficial consequences of involuntary askesis. How many times have we heard as we have visited a parishioner in the days following a heart attack, "It's the best thing that ever happened to me—I'll never be the same again. It woke me up to the reality of my life, to God, to what is important." Suddenly instead of mindlessly and compulsively pursuing an abstraction—success, or money, or happiness—the person is reduced to what is actually there, to the immediately personal—family, geography, body—and begins to live freshly in love and appreciation. The change is a direct consequence of a forced realization of human limits. Pulled out of the fantasy of a god condition and confined to the reality of the human condition, the person is surprised to be living not a diminished life but a deepened life, not a crippled life but a zestful life."[6]

Peterson's comments about unintentional askesis remind me of Andrew Sullivan, the most-read blogger in the world, and his observations about how HIV has changed his life. He says of contracting the disease:

My own sense is that it's the most important thing that's ever happened to me in my life. . . . It certainly helped me realize that careerism is idiotic. I had worked really hard and gotten to this place and then Boom! In one day I was told, "You're going to die, you can't stay in America and you'll probably have to quit your job. . . ." At that point you either go into denial and carry on as if it isn't happening, or you absorb it and have a life-changing moment. I mean who cares? I could be dead. . . . And then also the knowledge that God can strip you of everything, and what do you have left— it's a very useful moment in one's life to realize, what do I have if this is all taken away? What's left? What am I really living for? What are my values . . . ? It strips away a lot of stuff—if you let it. It's a place I came to die that taught me in a strange kind of way how to live. And I think that means letting go of a lot of stuff most of us are afraid to let go of.[7]

We're all familiar with the transformative power of these unintentional forms of askesis. While Sullivan's experience is an extreme example, there are other smaller, less dramatic encounters that nudge us toward clarity of mind and purpose. How many times have we heard people say that losing a job was the best thing that ever happened to them? Most of us can remember a romantic relationship that crushed us in disappointment, but in the end led to gratitude for more wide-open spaces. In big and small ways we know the rhythms of unintentional askesis.

Like Peterson, my role as a pastor has often given me a ringside seat to journey with people in the gift of these constraints. For example, I recently had the privilege of presiding over a beautiful but draining memorial service for a forty-five-year-old member of our church named Chrissy. I do around twenty memorial services a year—I've done as many as three in one week. In thirteen years of being a pastor, I have grown accustomed to the awkward rhythms of walking through the days and weeks that follow someone's death.

I've learned that when you die no one is going to talk about how successful you were or how much money you made. They will talk about your passions, and the volume of your laugh, and the things that brought you joy. They will mostly talk about the generosity of your love, or struggle with the lack thereof. They will rejoice in the miracle of reconciled relationships and sometimes carry wounds of unresolved resentments.

The service for Chrissy stands out as unique in my experience. My friend was diagnosed with a terminal brain tumor shortly before we started our year, only to have the cancer inexplicably disappear in 2008. For almost a year she lived in the grace moment of a miracle, and she lived it so well. She served and loved and seized life in the most wonderful ways. Tragically the cancer returned suddenly, and in a few short months she was gone. Her gift to me was the way she got me thinking about how I would live my life if I only had one year to live. What would I do if I were given the miracle of another year? And I guess that's the way it is, isn't it. We've all been given the miracle of another year, probably more but, then again, maybe not. We all live in that grace moment of a miracle every day, more often than not, unaware.

In the tradition of spiritual practices, askesis is an intentional effort to raise awareness of limitations. Peterson explains, "Askesis is voluntary disaster. . . . Why wait? Why wait for an accident, an illness, a failure? Why not take deliberate steps now to rid myself of the illusions of being a god, study the limits of my mortality, and sink myself into the quite marvelous but sin-obscured realities of creation and salvation?"[8]

In many ways our year of plenty was a voluntary disaster. It was a year of wonderful constraints. We grew very familiar with the questions, "Why not?" and "Why wait?"

We launched our efforts at intentional askesis in January, and the stock market collapsed in September. I vividly remember the day the market had its single largest one-day loss in history because that evening we gathered for the first of a series of informational meetings to raise money for renovations to the church. *Surreal* is a good way to describe how it felt.

I won't presume to speak for Nancy, but personally I felt surprisingly resilient in the face of the economic uncertainty. I found that my anxiety and fear of a personal financial catastrophe dissipated as we flexed the muscles of our resourcefulness. What if we lose our life savings and have to buy used shoes and socks from the local secondhand store? What if a new Depression befalls us, and we are forced to tear out the lawn, grow victory gardens, and can green beans like it was 1929? What if the dollar is devalued to the point that we are forced to resort to a bartering system with neighbors and farmers? What if it gets so bad we have to sell our cars and get around by walking and riding our bikes? I had a newfound suspicion that our family would find a way not only to survive but even thrive, come what may. I was learning that even if we had much less in the future, somehow it would be plenty.

In the end, the world economy seems to have survived our one family assault on the economic status quo. The stock market has rebounded and the commentators are once again sure that the best path forward is lots of consumer spending and long-term investment in the market. But our experiment did disrupt our family's financial life enough to see the wisdom in Wendell Berry's poetic advice at the beginning of this chapter. When it comes to our relationship with the global-industrial complex, he says: "So, friends, every day do something that won't compute. . . . Be like the fox who makes more tracks than necessary, some in the wrong direction. Practice resurrection." Trade minivans for elephant rides, the boredom of driving for the adventure of walking, faith in the future riches of a 401(k) for the hope of experiences here and now. In a world that glorifies unbounded freedom, take on meaningful constraints. These are the lessons we continue to learn.

CHAPTER 8

Close Encounters
of the Gardening Kind

*A garden that one makes oneself becomes associated with one's
personal history . . . interwoven with one's tastes, preferences,
and character, and constitutes a sort of unwritten, but withal
manifest, autobiography. Show me your garden, provided it be
your own, and I will tell you who you are.*[1]
—Alfred Austin

WHEN WE MOVED TO SPOKANE IN 2004, WE PURCHASED
a home in an established neighborhood near the Spokane
River, nestled in a fertile valley carved out by ice-age floods from
Lake Missoula. Driving up the main road to our winding hillside
neighborhood you pass a sign that touts it as a "Master Planned
Community," and over the last three decades the master plan has
filled the sloping ridge of decomposing granite with homes. Looking up the hill, there is a hard straight line running to the horizon marking where the development ends and the forest begins.
Our cedar-sided house has a normally proportioned front and back
yard by suburban standards, but in some 1980s-era loophole that
allowed pieces of land to remain unbuilt that today would certainly
have homes on them, it has a large side yard of about five thousand

square feet. It's a flat piece of land with direct sunlight, which is unusual for our neighborhood full of towering Ponderosa pines and precariously perched hillside homes. We purchased the house in August, and in a great bit of serendipity we inherited a small vegetable garden that bordered a large lawn area that covered most of the side yard.

The previous owners were kind enough to leave the bulk of vegetables for us to harvest and eat. For the first time in our lives we snapped green beans off at the stem and experienced their unique muffled crunch. We plucked vine-ripened, sun-soaked tomatoes and bit into them on the spot, juice dripping down our chins into the dark soil at our feet. We discovered the joy of monitoring the remarkable evolution of pumpkins from flower-capped nub to perfect green sphere to deeply ridged orange globe, all under a canopy of overlapping leaves, stems, and tangled tassels. Amid the chaos of renovating our house and adjusting to an unfamiliar community, the garden was a place of peace and security. We made regular outings to take in the wonder of food that is connected to plant and soil and place.

When spring rolled around the next year we took up the challenge to see if we could carry on the tradition of the vegetable garden. For the first time in my life I put a seed in the ground and waited for it to emerge from the soil. It seemed preposterous, like I was presuming to schedule a miracle or ask on demand for a mystery to reveal itself in plain sight.

The seed packs didn't help my lingering doubts. On the outside are glorious pictures of mature fruits and vegetables ready for eating. These pictures are such confidence boosters that on my inaugural visit to our local garden store I bought enough seed to plant a small farm. But my seed store confidence turned to bare dirt pessimism when I opened the seed packs to find dry, shriveled crumbs that appeared to have no meaningful relationship to the pictures on the seed packs. It seemed impossible that such small, inert morsels could give birth to life.

Despite my misgivings, I dove into planting the garden. Unable to imagine the size of the plants at full growth, I planted everything much too close—a classic mistake of first-time gardeners. I also didn't account for the need to access the plants once they were grown so that I could weed and harvest. I was creating the garden equivalent of a crowded Hong Kong city block. I also wasn't totally clear on the relationship between sunshine and food. I planted a whole batch of raspberry starts under the full shade of a silver maple tree, and it didn't dawn on me until much later when the vines looked stringy and pale that sun is actually really helpful for the production of fruit. And while I read in my gardening books that I couldn't expect my blueberry plants to give us a harvest until they had several years to develop the necessary root systems, I thought ours would surely be the exception. I was slightly offended that these books doubted my ability to overwhelm a plant with Miracle Gro and unwarranted optimism.

Along with stumbling through my own ineptitude, I had to learn to deal with the normal challenges gardeners face. On a small scale it seemed like we lived through every major agricultural disaster of the last two hundred years. There was blight on some of the potatoes and an invasion of morning glory and purslane weeds that reminded me of all the foreboding kudzu reports I heard on TV while growing up in North Carolina. There was an epidemic of ungerminated, still-born pumpkins that had me wondering if all of our area bee colonies had collapsed. In the early morning hours while the neighborhood slept, I was forced into the common but still shame-inducing, anatomically provocative practice of artificial inseminating my pumpkins. An infestation of earwigs led to a total harvest of two half-pollinated stalks of sweet corn. There were pheasants that loved to chop up seedlings with their beaks, not eating them, just decapitating the plants like a roving band of garden terrorists. There were freezes: late early freezes and early late freezes. At times I thought maybe there was a conspiracy against me, but over time I've come to see this as a normal year in the garden. As gardener poet Alfred Austin puts it, "There is no gardening without humility. Nature is constantly sending even its oldest scholars to the bottom of the class for some egregious blunder."[2]

Despite all of the challenges, the seedlings emerged from the dark soil, plants grew, fruit blossomed, and the garden, for the most part, thrived. While some things, like the corn, didn't materialize, we learned the virtues of the much-maligned zucchini plant that grows in our region like a noxious weed. It's the gardener's great fallback. When all else fails, the zucchini makes you feel like you could give P. Allen Smith a run for his money. Getting into the crowded garden to pluck the veggies felt a little like entering a jungle in need of a machete, but when all was said and done we had a successful first year.

It was a personal victory for me but it also marked a new era in our experience as a family. The girls were surprisingly engaged with what was happening in the garden. While they enjoyed the previous year's unearned harvest, there was something about seeing the plants emerge from bare soil that sparked their young imaginations. Midsummer, the children from the neighborhood made daily pilgrimages to the site of the garden, and along with playing their standard games like four square and torture the roly polys, they added "garden feasts" to their repertoire.

They roamed the rows of vegetable plants, gathering green beans, carrots, cucumbers, and whatever else was in season. They assembled their harvest on a plate, and like characters in an *Alice in Wonderland* tea party, they sat in a ritual circle on the grass and passed the plate of raw whole foods, eating them up like delicacies. When they started calling these ritual feasts "desserts" I feared we had unleashed some break in the space/time continuum of child rearing.

With each new growing season my interest and obsession with planting the garden grew. I started gathering seed packets like I collected baseball cards in the third grade. I bought lights and heat pads to start my own tomato and pepper plants. My neighbor joked that I'd better be careful not to attract the attention of law enforcement with my fleet of basement grow lights. Each year I found ways to expand the footprint of the garden. One year I added a fifty-foot-long, four-foot-high rock wall to make room for an herb garden. The next year I found space for a greenhouse. It seemed I had exhausted the reasonable and socially acceptable bounds of our vegetable growing—that is until we decided to transform the homegrown part of our lives from a hobby into an important source of nutrition.

Plowing Ahead

During the dark days of January 2008, I threw myself into planning our garden plot. Like never before, I negotiated ways to expand the area for growing food or at least maximize the space we already had. At some point I started entertaining the ridiculous possibility of tearing out the lawn and converting the whole yard into rows of vegetables. Our early experiments on the frontiers of local consumption had emboldened me, but somewhere in my as-yet unspoken deliberations about choosing food over lawns, I became aware of the invisible boundary of social acceptability. We lived with overt rules and ordinances, but we were testing the limits of the covert boundaries of suburban respectability. Like the speed-limit governor that school districts put on their buses to keep their bus drivers in check, there was a little voice in my head that kept asking the question, "What would the neighbors think?"

Our side yard buts up against a thoroughfare for neighborhood walkers. The large blue post office box on the corner along with the community mailbox means that a regular parade of cars stop to drop off and pick up their mail and all those folks look directly at our yard. In previous years I had relished the visibility of our reasonable and quaint vegetable garden, but I wasn't sure what they would think about a truck farm popping up in the neighborhood.

In fact, our experiment was revealing how our whole lives had been shaped by these questions about what neighbors and friends would think if we lived differently. How would they respond to my request for a ride home from a committee meeting because we only have one car? What would guests think about lentils and potatoes for dinner? What would Noel's friend think about getting a used antique doll for her birthday? How would our neighbors respond to chickens occasionally wandering into the street?

We committed many trespasses of perceived respectability during the year, but there was something about vandalizing the lawn that registered more severely on the scale of social anxiety. Maybe it goes back to the innovation of English lawns in the 1600s as status symbols among Jacobean aristocrats. The post-World War II proliferation of lawn mowers and fossil-fuel based chemical fertilizers have brought lush green lawns within the reach of most homeowners, but instead of indicating status they have evolved into a baseline of neighborhood decorum. Take a look at the typical homeowner's association rules for evidence:

> The Owner shall maintain the grounds and the improvements situated on each lot, including but not limited to, plantings, landscaping and lawns, at all times, in a neat and attractive manner satisfactory to the Association. PLEASE REMEMBER THAT THIS MEANS YOU NEED TO MAINTAIN YOUR LAWN. WEEDS ARE NOT CONSIDERED LAWN. PLEASE TRY TO MAINTAIN.[3]

The lawn is the bold-lettered baseline of neighborliness and stable property values. No wonder it felt like we were breaking a major norm just entertaining the idea of converting tidy green lawn into dirty looking dirt.

Our questioning of this unquestioned, and in some cases non-negotiable, norm led to some interesting discoveries. We learned that lawns are the largest irrigated agricultural "crop" in America. According to *Food Not Lawns: How to Turn Your Yard into a Garden and Your Neighborhood into a Community*, "Fifty-eight million Americans spend approximately 30 billion dollars every year to maintain more than 23 million acres of lawns. That's an average of over a third of an acre and $517 each. The same-sized plot of land could still have a small lawn for recreation and produce all the vegetables needed to feed a family of six. The lawns in the United States consume around 270 billion gallons of water a week—enough to water 81 million acres of organic vegetables all summer long."[4]

Could it be that a vegetable garden might be a better use of water and a more socially just, if not socially respectable, option? I was starting to see the virtues of food, not lawns, and combatted the prickles of social anxiety by thinking of it as a way to stick it to those snobby English aristocrats.

Our consumer lives were driven by social pressures. We dreaded the thought that someone would look down on us. We wanted to be good neighbors. We wanted to be liked. We wanted to be reputable. We wanted to fit in. We wanted to preserve our property value. But our new rules disarmed these implicit cultural norms in some wonderfully subversive ways. There was a whole new set of possibilities available to us. So one evening, while Noel and Lily watched TV, I sat on the couch with my gardening books on my lap plotting out the garden. I posed the question, "Girls, what would you think if we tore out the lawn on the side yard and made it all a vegetable garden?" Somehow I knew it was wise to ask them before bringing it up with Nancy.

They responded with eyes on the TV, half paying attention, "That sounds great Dad. Let's do it."

That was all the encouragement I needed. I scrapped my reasonably confined garden plot plan and drew up a new blueprint that included the whole side yard, four times the size of our existing garden plot. I doodled for a while thinking of how we might lay it out, and I asked the girls again, "What would you think if we made it into a labyrinth maze with a circle of grass in the middle?"

That got their attention and they gathered around to check out my picture of what our whole yard would look like if it were a vegetable garden maze.

"Wow, that looks great, Dad. We definitely have to do that," they both agreed.

With our enthusiasm growing, we walked up from the basement to present our idea to Nancy.

"What would you think if we tore out the lawn and put in a vegetable-garden labyrinth?" In retrospect that's a lot for a spouse to take in out of the blue. I maybe should have broken it to her slowly like I did with the girls, but we were downright giddy with ourselves and couldn't contain our enthusiasm.

Nancy rolled her eyes and said, "Ummmmm. That sounds nice, whatever." Her unspoken words, "Yeah right, like that will ever happen."

It wasn't until a week later when I came home with a sod cutter that her bemused indifference turned to genuine concern.

"You're not really going to do that, are you?" she said. "Where will the girls play? What will the neighbors think? Think about all the weeds? We can hardly keep up with the garden we already have."

I assured her, "It's going to be great. The girls are really excited about it, and if we're going to make it through this year we need to grow as much food as we can. Trust me."

It probably wasn't the best marital compromise ever reached. I agreed to take full responsibility for the garden, and she agreed to not look at what we were doing out there. As Nancy says, it was the equivalent of putting her hands over her ears and saying, "La, La, La, La, I'm not listening to you."

That night when Noel got back from school, we went out and fired up the sod cutter. Like a giant rolling cheese slicer, the cutter glided over the dormant lawn. You couldn't really tell the grass had been cut until we started rolling it up from one end to the other like a sixty-foot-long green sleeping bag. After rolling up a couple of rows of the soggy sod, it became apparent that it was going to take some significant work to pull this off. One small roll of sod weighed upwards of fifty pounds. And we had to sort out where to put it all.

Nancy joked that we could pile it up in the living room like Richard Dreyfus did in *Close Encounters of the Third Kind*. She said, "You know, when he went absolutely crazy and lost his grip on reality." I was sure I wasn't going crazy, and despite Nancy's doubts, I had a feeling my grip on reality had never been better.

What Grows in the Garden

It has always made intuitive sense to me that spending time out in the garden is good for my health and general well being, especially for reducing stress. It turns out there may be a scientific basis for such a claim. A recent study on the effects of exposure to a common soil bacteria called mycobacterium vaccae shows a strong correlation between the bacteria and improved learning and lowered anxiety. Injecting the bacteria into mice has been shown to increase serotonin levels and decrease anxiety. Researchers wondered if it might have a subsequent effect on learning. They fed the bacteria to mice and then tested them in a maze. Lo and behold, these mice navigated the maze twice as fast as mice who received no bacteria. So when we're out digging in the dirt, it's likely that we're breathing in this bacteria and when we eat food like carrots dug up from healthy soil it's likely we're getting a good dose of mycobacterium vaccae.

The benefits of gardening and turning a lawn into a vegetable garden can't be entirely summed up by the science. Talk to a dozen gardeners and you might get a dozen different reasons why gardening is a life-giving act. They might point out that recently harvested vegetables have much higher nutritional content than vegetables sitting on store shelves for weeks. They might point out that there's nothing like the taste of a vine-ripened tomato and a freshly plucked and sliced kohlrabi. For some it's the earthy connection of hands sunk in the soil, and for others gardening is an abiding connection with their childhood on the farm. Some might bring up the economics of growing your own food, saying it saves money. I've always been a little suspicious of this logic.

People often ask me if I will ever sell my vegetables at the farmers' market. I am quick to point out that because of all the time spent and garden gadgets purchased I'd have to charge $20 per tomato to make any money on them. Author William Alexander did a detailed analysis of the actual cost of his first year's garden harvest of nineteen Brandywine heirloom tomatoes, an analysis that led to the book, *The $64 Tomato: How One Man Nearly Lost His Sanity, Spent a Fortune, and Endured and Existential Crisis in the Quest for the Perfect Garden.* So maybe my $20 is optimistic. Despite my skepticism I do know home gardeners who through a disciplined regimen of composting, mulching, and crop rotation are able to produce a small fortune's worth of fresh fruits and vegetables for almost nothing. To them I say, "I'm not worthy."

Gardening taps into something primal in me, the hunter/gatherer part of my brain. When I walk in the house with arms full of freshly dug potatoes, there is part of me that wants to toss the harvest down on the kitchen counter in front of Nancy, grunting and pounding my chest in a display of virility that lets everyone in the vicinity know that I'm a good provider for our growing family. I don't know if Nancy would be impressed by such a display, but I'm sure she'd agree that it's better than pulling into the driveway with a dead moose on the hood of our car. She'll take the gatherer over the hunter any day.

You ask any gardener, and they have their reasons.

Our garden labyrinth introduced me to a new motivation for gardening, or at least helped me understand a reason that had been stirring in me for quite some time—that gardening for me is a spiritual practice, a fertile field of formation, an encounter with divine rhythms.

When we settled on the design of our lawn-turned-vegetable-garden, I had inklings of walking a labyrinth as a spiritual practice. I was aware of its use in medieval Christianity and that it was experiencing a resurgence in some faith communities. I used the design of the famous maze built into the floor of the Chartres Cathedral in France with its four quadrants as the model for our garden. I would come to understand those quadrants as a symbol of our journey through the four seasons.

Little is written about the use of labyrinths in the medieval church, but we do know they emerged as alternatives to making a pilgrimage to Jerusalem. Instead of navigating the Crusade-riddled pathways from Europe to the Middle East, Christians were invited to a pilgrimage in their own backyards, an enacted metaphor of the journey to God, a microexpedition that takes twists and turns, moves toward God and away, that incorporates being lost and being found, being dead in the outer reaches and alive at the center. It's a place where seemingly fragmented, haphazard pathways come together as an intentional journey, all bounded by the fold of God's grace.

While I knew the design held provocative potential, it was more of a whim than an intentional embrace of ancient prayer walks. I figured it was a good way to get the kids to buy into giving up prime space for running and rolling in the grass. But ultimately it did help me connect the dots between digging in the garden and seeking after God. In the tradition of the ancients, it was for me a place for quiet reflection and centering. And it was a vegetable garden with the everyday urgencies of weeds and aphids and ordinary wonders of crisp cucumbers and colorful mallows. It was gardening as spiritual practice, a place of integration, soil and spirit, heaven and earth, holiness and humus. I was coming to know the garden as a place of formation, the kind of formation Matthew Crawford describes in his book *Shop Class as Soul Craft: An Inquiry into the Value of Work.*

Crawford is a Ph.D. turned motorcycle mechanic. In his book, he writes about his experience as a mechanic and the way technical work can free us from the narcissistic fog of predetermined consumer choices that dominate our lives. He says:

> As every parent knows, infants think the world revolves around them, and everything ought to be instantly available to them. At an earlier stage of technological progress, I am sure that contending with a motorcycle, like contending with the farm animals that likely inhabited the same barn as the motorcycle, helped along the process of becoming an adult. When your shin gets kicked, whether by a mule or a kick-starter, you get schooled. It would be strange to pine for the inconvenience of old motorcycles. They truly are a pain in the #$@. My point rather is to consider the moral significance of material culture. . . . On all sides, we see fewer occasions for the exercise of judgment. . . . For the one who takes on the yoke of working with a mule or a motorcycle, his will is educated—both chastened and focused—so it no longer resembles that of a raging baby who knows only what he wants. Both as workers and as consumers, technical education seems to contribute to moral education.[5]

These mechanical arts shape and conform us to the unbending mechanics of their design. Instead of self-centered obsessions with ourselves, we are forced to deal with and be attentive to something beyond our making. According to Crawford, this plays a key role in moral formation, and from my perspective it is also at the heart of spiritual formation.

In some ways, farming, gardening, and seed starting are an even better manual practice for nurturing the soul. Instead of just connecting us to the created motorcycle, it forces us to engage the whole created order of things—earth and sun and seasons. It's a kind of education, a cultivator of otherwise unattended virtues.

That's how Wendell Berry describes the act of gardening in his book, *A Continuous Harmony: Essays Cultural and Agricultural*. Of all the things he can think of to help get people personally involved in the care of the environment, he recommends gardening. He reasons,

> A person who undertakes to grow a garden at home, by practices that will preserve rather than exploit the economy of the soil, has set his mind decisively against what is wrong with us. He is helping himself in a way that dignifies him and that is rich in meaning and pleasure. But he is doing something else that is more important; He is making vital contact with the soil and the weather on which his life depends. He will no longer look upon rain as a traffic impediment, or upon the sun as a holiday decoration.[6]

According to Berry, gardening can be a powerful tool in forming people, in waking us up to our surroundings and moving us to action. It is, at its core, an integrative act. He says that our experience in the garden will help us to

> see that beauty and utility are alike dependent upon the health of the world. . . . We will see that war and oppression and pollution are not separate issues, but are aspects of the same issue . . . .. We will know that no person is free except in the freedom of other persons,

and that our only freedom is to know and faithfully occupy our place—a much humbler place than we have been taught to think—in the order of creation.[7]

As I carved curvaceous pathways into the large expanse of newly unveiled bare dirt in our yard, I had a giddy sense that we were somehow more faithfully occupying our place in the order of creation. A patch of lawn that in previous summers was the scene of epic battles with tenacious weeds and chronic dry patches of brown was becoming a place of formation, both a training ground for the journey and a living metaphor of pilgrimage to the Creator: Father, Son, and Holy Spirit.

In a positive sign for the future of our marriage, Nancy joined me in the task of removing sod and hauling manure. And in another sign of progress, we weren't too concerned about the growing buzz among the neighbors peering over the mailbox wondering what in the world was going on at the Goodwin house.

III: Summer

"As long as the earth endures,
seedtime and harvest,
cold and heat,
summer and winter,
day and night
will never cease."
—Gen. 8:22

O NE NIGHT AFTER DINNER, I OBSERVED AN EXTRA-
ordinary exchange between Nancy and Noel. They were
discussing school lunches, and I heard Noel say, "Mommy can I
pleeeeease have asparagus in my lunch tomorrow?"

This might have been some kind of strange milestone in childhood development or it could have been the early stages of some
childhood dementia or delusions brought on by severe malnutri-
tion. Whatever it was, it made me realize I would have to adjust my
usual parenting instincts for bragging and gushing about my kids.
It would go something like this:

Fellow Parent: "My daughter has been accepted into the gifted
program and wants to be an astronaut when she grows up."

Me: "How wonderful. My daughter wants asparagus in her
school lunch. Top that."

As May turned to June, we unloaded the greenhouse. Like
abruptly tipping over a bucket that had been slowly filling with
water until it was near overflowing, we tipped the greenhouse over,
flooding the garden rows with plant after plant after plant. We dug

in thirty tomato starts, burying the majority of the hairy stems under the soil, knowing that every hair would be transformed into a nutrient-absorbing root. Next to the tomatoes we inserted large-leaf basil—combinations that taste good together on the dinner plate usually go well together in the garden. We planted thirty pepper plants, lined up in formation, tucked in close, comforting each other with elbowed leaves brushing against each other—they don't like to be alone. I took our tender squash plants and gently put them in hills. They don't like to have their roots tussled like most plants. They are so sensitive.

I started planting seeds in February, and now, almost five months later, the greenhouse was empty, and all the plants were in the ground. What used to be grass was now a complex garden maze with raised-bed rows built up like a half-submerged snake winding its way around the whole yard in a coil. The sun was shining, and the soil was heating up. Our confidence was growing. Then, on June 11, disaster struck.

It was a hot day at the farmers' market, and as is typical for that time of year, turbulent clouds formed in the distance, stirred up by rising and falling combinations of hot and cold air. These usually didn't amount to much, and after living for seven years in the chaos of Houston's gulf-coast weather, Spokane's weather seemed mild as can be. So it was a real surprise when upon returning home from the market, the sky turned tornado green and in a sudden rush of ice and lightning, unleashed the Kraken.

I screamed out to no one in general, "The garden!" and ran through the garage into the garden, grabbing a large blue tarp on the way. I got out into the middle of the labyrinth to find that an inch of penny-sized hailstones and rain had already filled the bottom of the pathways. I've never felt closer to lightning than in that moment with flashes of light crackling around me. Just as quickly as I ran into the garden in a terror fearing for my pepper plants, I ran out of the garden fearing for my life. I made it back in the house, completely drenched, unable to cover any of our tender plants. Already in mourning, Nancy and I gathered by the window as the storm carried on for another five minutes, relentlessly pummeling everything into the ground. It was the biggest hailstorm. Ever.

Given the drumming noise of the hail pounding the earth and the destructive finality of its force, the aftermath of the storm was strangely calm. Just outside the front door, I had some pumpkin starts in pots, not yet planted. As I ventured down the porch, I could see their now naked stems pointing up out of the pots, their once broad leaves shredded on the ground like pumpkin shrapnel. The little valleys of the garden pathways were now filled all the way to the top, six inches deep with standing water and floating ice. The sloping ridges of the rows looked like they had just received a fresh coat of popcorn ceiling. The vertical stems were all that remained of the peppers. The leaves of the tomato plants were shot through with holes like someone had been hunting for turkeys in the garden. The one surprise gift of the storm was that for the first time the labyrinth design was completely visible, the path set off by a line of brown dirt just below the ice-capped beds and just above the moat that now filled the pathways. It was beautiful.

Thankfully most of our plants bounced back. Green leaves emerged from the mysterious place between the vertical stem and the stripped branches of the peppers. Our tomatoes rebounded, adding a new forest of green leaves to replace the chopped and chipped leftovers from the storm. Our squash plants were a total loss, but I had a couple leftovers in the greenhouse along with the cucumbers I hadn't planted yet. The storm happened early enough that our garden was able to make a comeback, which was more than the cherry orchard up the road could say. Wood's Cherries, the last remaining orchard on Orchard Prairie, lost their whole year's harvest, a one-shot-only, year-in-the-making crop, gone in five minutes.

For five months, the greenhouse and garden disciplined me, requiring daily nonnegotiable attention with watering and fertilizing. That spring, not a day went by without attending in one way or another to the land and the weather. On cold days I had to make sure the greenhouse was heated just right or the delicate plants inside would freeze. On hot days I had to prop up the window vents or everything would shrivel.

I was learning to pay attention to the environment around me like never before, the rhythms of a life in relationship with the land and seasons. The garden was my mentor and task master. It was an apprenticeship in creation, and the hailstorm brought the hardest of lessons. Ultimately, nature and the environment are beyond my control. Collaborating with the land requires humility and respect. Even my most successful harvests are an act of mercy, not a triumph of will but a sign of grace. And if that's true for my harvests it's true for all the harvests. Everything on the shelves at the grocery store and on the tables at the farmers' market, everything in my refrigerator at home and on my plate at the dinner table, everything is a miracle of grace.

The hailstorm taught me that sometimes all I can do is throw my hands up in the air and acknowledge that I am at the mercy of forces greater than myself. I have to let the Babel tower of human ambition crash to pieces in front of me and accept that I am a subject and not a master in the created order of things.

CHAPTER 9

Master Food Preserver/ Master *of* Divinity

Perhaps the greatest disaster of human history is one that happened to or within religion: that is, the conceptual division between the holy and the world, the excerpting of the Creator from the creation. . . . and this split in public attitudes was inevitably mirrored in the lives of individuals: A man could aspire to heaven with his mind and his heart while destroying the earth, and his fellow men, with his hands.[1]
—Wendell Berry

M Y FAVORITE POSTER OF THE WWI ERA DEPICTS A YOUNG woman in an apron with ruffled sleeves. She is leaning back with her eyes wide and her arms stretched out in a precarious embrace of quart jars of canned vegetables, all under the proclamation, "Of Course I Can! I'm Patriotic as Can Be." Other posters of the genre expand on this call to arms/jars, featuring red, white, and blue kitchen aprons with headlines like, "Are you a Victory Canner?" or "Can Vegetables, Fruits, and the Kaiser Too." Poor Kaiser Wilhelm not only had to step down from leading Germany after WWI, but he was symbolically water bathed in a quart jar along with a batch of pickles by an army of American women.

Like most people of my generation, my only experience with food preservation came from grandparents who grew up in the era of these posters. They lived their childhood years in the scarcity of the Great Depression and their young adult years in the urgency of World War II. They planted victory gardens and stocked root cellars with the summer's harvest to ensure enough for the long winter months. Hot steamy days in the kitchen were empowered with the urgency that comes with grand battles between good and evil, survival and death. I grew up being told to clean my plate because there were starving children in China. My grandparents grew up being told to can more green beans because the fate of world depended on it.

I started the year lamenting that we hadn't spent the whole summer leading up to our experiment canning local fruits and vegetables. So when I saw a Master Food Preserver Class advertised through our local county extension office, I signed up right away. The title of the class was alluring. It made it feel like I was signing up for some intriguing eastern religion course in miracles with a survivalist edge. They actually changed the handbook title to a more antiseptic sounding, "Food Safety Advisor Volunteer," but that didn't stop any of us from sticking with the exotic title that made us all men and women of mystery.

I rode my bike to the first class with a great sense of expectation. I walked through the county extension office doors and into an exercise in "one of these things is not like the others." There were thirty women, and three men. Dave, the sausage prophet from the Millwood Farmers' Market, had his eye on making jam to sell at the markets. He was there on business. When I asked the other man, an older gentleman, what drew him to the class, he explained that his wife was looking for ways to get him out of the house and had insisted he attend.

The women in the class included nurses, a food editor from the local newspaper, and small-scale farmers looking for value-added strategies to sell products at the farmers' markets, all of them veterans of canning and food preservation. Then there was me, a thirty-nine-year-old Presbyterian pastor with a sixth-grade home economics class and some runny canned salsa on my culinary resume.

I certainly don't mean to be sexist in highlighting the gender of my classmates, as if women of course belonged there because food preservation is women's work. The basic economics of the home have changed dramatically in the last fifty years, but this class felt like stepping back into a time gone by, when women (yes it was almost always women) worked relentlessly through the heat of summer, canning fruits and vegetables. It was stepping back into an heirloom practice, which was at one time a necessary part of making it through winter, to a time when there was a community canning kitchen that would take the fresh harvest of summer and process it for you.

It took me back in more personal ways, connecting me to flavors and textures of childhood experiences with my grandmother who had a garage half filled with boxes of canning jars and white-speckled, blue-enameled canning tubs. Every year she supplied us with exotic jars of raspberry jam, the tops covered in waxy paraffin. I remember sticking the knife into the paraffin and scooping it out like a shifting iceberg, eager to get a taste of the seed-speckled red fruit.

This feeling of stepping back was part of the appeal. It gave an empowering sense of self-sufficiency. It was old school and vintage, out of practice just long enough to make it hip. But there was something else running more deeply through my life as I sharpened my pencil to take notes on the acidity levels of vegetables and the proper blanching techniques for freezing foods. It was something that had been brewing and maturing in me for quite some time.

At the time I'd been a pastor for almost twelve years. About five years into my vocational journey, I found myself suffocating within the dualistic divide that gets handed to you when you are called a "Master of the Divine." Yes, upon graduating from seminary they give you a diploma with the words, "Master of Divinity" emblazoned over your name. It isn't intended to suggest that seminary students have learned to "master" all things divine, but it does unintentionally point to the practical realities of being a pastor. In a world that is divided up into the categories of sacred and secular, spiritual and material, earthly and heavenly, pastors are more often than not assigned by churches to attend to spiritual realities and divine truths. On top of that it's common for pastors like myself to pick up the idea along the way that it's the spiritual that really matters, the heavenly that's most important. By implication, the material/secular things of the world are secondary concerns. This honestly is part of the appeal of becoming a pastor, or at least it was for me. In a divided world with one side lifted up as more important than the other, it felt virtuous to choose the weightier side of the equation.

So pastors end up saying pious things like, "Our greatest fear should not be fear of failure but a fear of succeeding in things that have no eternal impact," as if there are things that have nothing to do with the eternal or divine, corners of the world where holiness and faithfulness are inaccessible and irrelevant. When describing efforts at social justice we make statements like, "Before we feed people's souls we need to feed their bodies," as if the one is completely disconnected from the other and that in some imposition of geometry on the order of the universe, these dualisms are in linear sequence.

After years of living within the pressure cooker of the faux meaningfulness of this sacred/secular divide, I had begun to acknowledge that it just wasn't true. The world as I experienced it is not neatly divided up into these categories. And more than that, the God I follow in Jesus is much harder to nail down than I imagined, showing up in the most unlikely places. It also isn't true that the substance of my vocation is somehow more important. In fact I had a sneaking suspicion that the rhythms of my vocation were very often leading me to miss out on what really matters. Far from the expansive hopefulness that launched me into the ministry, the incessant focus on what happens in a sanctuary for a couple hours every Sunday seemed like a small world and a small vocation.

Many, if not most, people find themselves on the other side of this great divide, assuming a sacred/secular chasm and feeling trapped in the crass materiality of the world, longing for more meaning. In a strange and confusing twist, I found myself on the opposite side, drowning in meaningfulness, suffocating in an incessant focus on the eternal.

I can relate in some ways to Elizabeth Gilbert in her book, *Eat, Pray, Love*, where she describes her journey out of materialism into a spiritual quest for the transcendent, only my journey is in reverse. On the occasion of her first prayer, Gilbert writes:

> Something was about to occur on that bathroom floor that would change forever the progression of my life—almost like one of those crazy astronomical super-events when a planet flips over in outer space for no reason whatsoever, and its molten core shifts, relocating its poles and altering its shape radically, such that the whole mass of the planet suddenly becomes oblong instead of spherical. Something like that.
>
> What happened was I started to pray.
>
> You know—like, to God.[2]

For me, instead of reaching out of the secular abyss toward heaven, I found myself moving away from the constant focus on the transcendent to sink my hands into the holy materiality of the world. That has been my pole-shifting, planet-flipping experience. My version sounds something like this:

Something was about to happen in my Master Food Preserver class that would change forever the progression of my life. What happened is I learned how to make chutney and can salmon.

You know—like fish.

It doesn't quite have the intrigue of prayer, but this would be among my transformational practices. It was part of my slow but sure movement away from the grandiosity of mastering the divine toward the skills of paying attention to the fruits of the earth, the wonder of the everyday, the incarnate God who defies our dualisms by proclaiming all things important, all things worthy of redemption, all things caught up in the drama of resurrection. While Elizabeth Gilbert was on an exotic journey toward Eastern mysticism, I was becoming my grandmother.

AN ORDINARY KINGDOM

Our family's focus on all things local got me interested in issues that would have slid right by me before. For example, I took note of an article about the rising demand for farmland in the Seattle area and another story about folks in Missoula, Montana, organizing to stop subdivisions. The presenting issue in both stories was the current pressure to localize food sources. I was learning that the issue of food quickly becomes an issue of land. When we start paying attention to where our food comes from, we start paying attention to what we do with the land around us. We had certainly experienced this in a small way with our change in land-use policy at the Goodwin residence.

A few years ago I used a quote in the church newsletter from Wendell Berry's collection of essays, *Standing by Words*. (I know at this point it's hard for you to imagine me using a quote from Wendell Berry.) He says:

> It invariably turns out, I think, that one's first vision of one's place was to some extent an imposition on it. But if one's sight is clear and one stays on and works well, one's love gradually responds to the place as it really is, and one's visions gradually image possibilities that are really in it.[3]

At the time, I wrote of it as a metaphor for our church sorting through the possibilities for ministry on our corner of the block, in our unique place in the community. I still love it as a community-development metaphor, but given my renewed perspectives, I love it now more as it was intended, as wisdom for the use of real land in real places.

Maybe this is a helpful way to describe some of the changes that were happening in me. I became less interested in metaphors for living, and more interested in just living. I was less interested in the metaphor of the garden and more interested in the actual dirt in my backyard. I was less interested in the worn out pep talk metaphors of risk taking, and more interested in buying tickets to Thailand with our insurance check. I was less interested in the metaphor of love, and more interested in real loving actions with real people in real places. My abstract conceptions of holiness gave way to what some might call an earthy spirituality. I'd been snookered into thinking that the metaphors and the ideas would give me access to the sacred spaces, but I was learning that the simple, tangible act of buying something—or not—is a sacred event itself, an access point into the kingdom of God.

I wrote about the slow move toward earthiness and my increasing wariness of abstractions on our blog. It provoked some interesting responses from friends who read the post. Keith wrote, "Action or metaphor, both are empty without love, no? Without wisdom, action and metaphor, however well intentioned, are impotent, at worst leading to chaos and blindness."

Karen wrote:

So Craig's assertion that he is less interested in metaphor and more interested in just living is—sorry, Craig—not quite the whole story. In order to live in the intentional way he's chosen, he needed to have a way to describe that choice. Metaphor, philosophy, purpose statement, whatever you call it, that's where it starts. Only within that language framework do the choices make sense. So I'd suggest in fact that what's happening in Craig's garden is not that he's giving up on metaphor, and by association on wisdom, but that the frame and the fact are coming into alignment in a way that makes them feel like one and the same thing—that makes them feel true.

Karen and Keith were both right about the bigger picture including both meaning/metaphor and action working in harmony. They were also right that I was reacting against those two being falsely torn asunder. A big part of our year was to somehow put them back together in a way that was truthful.

I should clarify that I was not pushing back against all meaning or abstraction or metaphor. These symbolic structures of meaning are all around us and within us even if we don't acknowledge them. As Christians we sum up our framework of meaning as the kingdom of God. I believe it is this kingdom that has come in Jesus, and it is this kingdom that beckons us into the future, even as it comes at us. This kingdom is more real, more solid, and truthful than any other so-called kingdom that would claim my allegiance. I lead worship every Sunday hoping that our congregation, in the midst of divided allegiances, will be caught up in the meanings and metaphors and symbols of this kingdom of God.

The question that has been nagging at me is about how we get at the kingdom of God. The Bible, despite our common use of the phrase, never describes the kingdom as something we build or bring. It is never described as a project we initiate. Our relationship to the kingdom is always framed in terms of us entering or receiving.[4] It is something already going on that we relate to and respond to. It requires a certain attentiveness.

And this is where I find the struggle. Too often we confuse attentiveness with separating ourselves from our everyday lives in order to "make room for God." I read the pitch for a summer camp that says, "Our lives are so busy it's hard to hear what God has to say. Come away for the weekend and let God speak to you." The subtle assumption is that the actual experience of everyday living is not good raw material for hearing God speak. As a hungry soul who longs for God, this pitch tells me that the best I can hope for is a weekend away, a momentary encounter to tide me over.

In this way the church often resembles what philosopher Zygmunt Bauman calls "carnival communities." Such communities he says, "offer temporary respite from the agonies of daily solitary struggles . . . and like philosophy in Ludwig Wittgenstein's melancholy musings, they 'leave everything as it was.'"[5] The story of the kingdom claims that in the end nothing is left as it was. Everything is renewed and redeemed. So why is everything, despite our best poetic efforts, more often than not, left "as it was"?

Part of my diagnosis is that while Christians claim ultimate allegiance to the story of the kingdom, there is another story, another metaphor, that trumps all the others: the metaphor of the individual consumer. While we grasp and flail for other, more truthful frameworks for living, our social imagination is captive to the idea of the autonomous chooser of goods and services. Even when we try to see ourselves as responsible members of a community of mutual love, we have drunk so deeply from the well of self-interest that these images are stillborn, never really having a chance to settle in and do their necessary mischief in our daily lives.

So back to my question: How might we, in the midst of these swirling circumstances, get at the kingdom of God? My emerging answer is that we need to more attentively enter the actual circumstances of our lives. Don't give me a retreat or an expert or a book or a new gadget to better organize my finances and make me a more efficient consumer. Don't give me metaphors that in a backward way only serve to reinforce the prevailing wisdom, whose veiled purpose is to leave everything as it was. Instead, give me skills and practices that nurture awareness of truth in the midst of these circumstances.

Our year was about entering our lives as consumers, seeking awareness, trying not to let any purchase escape our attentiveness. If God's kingdom is indeed going on in the world, then the answer is not to remove ourselves from a life of consuming, but rather to enter it as if we were entering the kingdom, as if we love and care for our neighbors, as if welcoming a stranger is like welcoming Jesus, as if all of God's creation is good as God proclaimed it in Genesis 2, as if there is enough for everyone, as if all of God's creation is swept up in the drama of God's redeeming work in Jesus Christ.

And in this entering, we become poetic miners[6] of God's kingdom, listening to the emerging story, and hopefully giving it a voice; the kingdom of God is like a farmers' market, the kingdom of God is like a CSA box, the kingdom of God is like a farm with happy chickens, the kingdom of God is like. . . . That's how Jesus entered and told and enacted the story. That is my understanding of how we also are called to enter the world.

And that's why I joined the Master Food Preserver class.

Plus, I really like homemade salsa.

SOUL PRESERVER

In his book *Descartes' Bones: A Skeletal History of the Conflict between Faith and Reason*, Russell Shorto does as good a job as any contemporary writer in describing the roots of the dualistic divides that animate our modern lives. He traces the origins back to philosopher Rene Descartes and Descartes' intentional separation of the sacred and secular. Shorto writes,

> By stressing a dualistic view of reality, by putting the ephemeral stuff of mind and soul in one category and the physical world in another, [Descartes] believed he was building a wall around the fortress of faith, protecting it from the encroachments of science. At the same time, he was hoping to protect investigations of the natural world from theological interference.[7]

Descartes pioneered explorations of the physical, material world through the scientific method and felt that the only way to protect his devout faith in these explorations was to envision a world with two distinct spheres of logic and influence.

Shorto's description of this often-elusive philosophical debate comes with a wonderfully provocative living metaphor to go along with his historical analysis. It turns out that some time after Descartes' death, his skull became separated from his body. Just as Shorto chronicles the quandary of this philosophical divide between mind and body, he narrates the real world quandary of reuniting Descartes' physical head with his physical body. In a fitting twist, today the skull is housed in a science museum while the skeletal remains of his body are housed in a church.

In Shorto's analysis, not only has the quest to reunite Descartes' head with his body failed, but the efforts to bridge this divide in the modern world are as yet inconclusive. Shorto concludes,

> The hard fact of modernity is that from the time that Descartes separated the two, nobody has yet come up with a definitive way to solder mind and brain together again. Descartes declared in 1646 that it may not be possible. In 1998, Thomas Nagel stated flatly that "no one has a plausible answer to mind-body problems."[8]

The discontent with the divide between body and spirit that I've experienced in my pastoral vocation isn't a reflection on the churches or the people I've pastored. It's not some deficiency in my seminary education or the skills of those who mentored me in the faith. It's a discontent that stirs deeply in the modern era without prejudice. Like the air we breathe, we hardly notice the ways that we assume the world's dualisms, and most of the time we hardly realize how badly we suffer under their false imposition on our lives.

Where Shorto has yet to find an answer, I have found the Bible to be a great comfort and resource, a hopeful place of integration, especially Paul's introductory words in the book of Colossians where he writes:

> The Son is the image of the invisible God, the firstborn over all creation. For in him all things were created: things in heaven and on earth, visible and invisible, whether thrones or powers or rulers or

authorities; all things have been created through him and for him. He is before all things, and in him all things hold together. And he is the head of the body, the church; he is the beginning and the firstborn from among the dead, so that in everything he might have the supremacy. For God was pleased to have all his fullness dwell in him, and through him to reconcile to himself all things, whether things on earth or things in heaven, by making peace through his blood, shed on the cross. (Col. 1:15-20)

It's helpful to remember that in Paul's day there were influential philosophers, called the Gnostics, who concluded that the divisions between body and spirit were irreconcilable. Paul casts a comprehensive vision that stands as a very compelling answer to the supposedly intractable divides of his day. His vision of the cosmic Christ redeeming all things is as timely today as it was in the first century.

As Dr. Rich Mouw points out, there certainly are places in the Bible where "the world" is portrayed in a negative light. John says we must not "love the world or anything in the world" (1 John 2:15), but the same John also records the words, "For God did not send his Son into the world to condemn the world, but to save the world through him" (John 3:17). We are warned of evil in the world, but we are assured that despite this, God loves the world and is redeeming the world in his Son, Jesus. I like the way Mouw describes our participation in God's love of the world as "holy worldliness."[9]

Attending the Master Food Preserver class was part of my experiment in holy worldliness. After eight weeks of learning how to make pickles, sauerkraut, jams, and jellies along with being sufficiently terrorized by the possibility of killing my family if I didn't follow the recipes in the books, I received my Master Food Preserver certificate. I took my certificate back to the office, put it in a frame and hung it on the wall next to my master of divinity degree.

A friend came by the office that week and when he saw the unlikely pairing on the wall he said, "You know that's the perfect match. Your job as a pastor is to preserve people's souls. Is that what you mean by hanging that up there? Are you saying that you're a 'soul canner'?"

I replied, "That's not quite what I had in mind. It's my way of saying that God is in the midst of redeeming all things, and I'm doing my best to pay attention to and be a part of what God is doing."

The disconnect between spiritual truth and the material world is as much a sickness of modernity as it is of religion. My intent here is not to bash religion—I am grateful for my conversion to Christ, I love being a pastor, and have great hope for the church. My observation here is more personal lament than global outrage, more about spiritual formation than apologetics.

For us, tearing out the lawn, finding local food sources, meeting the people who make what we consume was, at least in part, an experiment in reweaving faith and soil, earthy reality and divine truth, backyard and baptismal font.

At the same time, this desire for holism changed my perspective as a pastor. The church in North America seems to have signed a long-term endorsement deal with modernity and its dualisms that looked like the deal of the century for a while but has taken a tragic turn where people feel like they have to choose between spirituality and a community of faith. I'm thinking of a friend who no longer attends church because she says she experiences God in nature. I'm thinking of the growing crowds of people who say they are spiritual but not religious. I see this as more a rejection of the false divide of the "holy and the world" than it is a rejection of God. So I am experimenting with what it looks like to lead a church that rejects this false divide and witnesses to a holistic faith. I do the normal stuff like preach and visit the hospital and write newsletter articles, but I also manage a farmers' market and help distribute food with Second Harvest and work to establish community gardens in our neighborhood and write a blog about local food.

And let me be as clear as I can: my interest in food and consumption is not some bait-and-switch effort to slip Jesus into people's lives, as if local food were some carrot on a stick to lead people along into the holy. The whole point is that I am learning to pay attention to real carrots, preferably local and organic, and see them as holy in some way. If I am seeking to convert people, it is a conversion to a whole life where truth and holiness are wedded to earthiness. At least that's the ongoing conversion I'm seeking in my own life.

CHAPTER 10

Chicken Dignity

The pleasure of eating should be an extensive pleasure, not that of the mere gourmet. People who know the garden in which their vegetables have grown and know that the garden is healthy will remember the beauty of the growing plants, perhaps in the dewy first light of morning when gardens are at their best. Such a memory involves itself with the food and is one of the pleasures of eating. The knowledge of good health of the garden relieves and frees and comforts the eater. The same goes for eating meat. The thought of the good pasture and of the calf contentedly grazing flavors the steak. Some, I know, will think this bloodthirsty or worse to eat a fellow creature you have known all its life. On the contrary, I think it means that you eat with understanding and with gratitude. A significant part of the pleasure of eating is in one's accurate consciousness of the lives and the world from which food comes.[1]
—Wendell Berry

THE BASIC PREMISE OF OUR EXPERIMENT WAS HUMAN dignity and the belief that it is important to know and care for the people involved in bringing our food and other products to market. But as I learned about the processes of bringing meat to market, I was reminded that I needed to add another dimension of dignity to our premise: chicken dignity.

Rich Mouw, one of my professors and mentors from seminary, highlights this kind of dignity in his book, *Praying at Burger King*. In the book he describes a gathering of Mennonite and Dutch Reformed farmers where one farmer is particularly upset about the treatment of chickens and the push of industrial farming practices. As Mouw tells it, the disgruntled farmer stood up and announced,

> Colonel Sanders wants us to think of chickens in terms of dollars and cents. They are nothing but little pieces of meat to be bought and sold for food. And so we're supposed to crowd them together in small spaces and get them fat enough to be killed. . . . But that's wrong! the Bible says that God created every animal 'after its own kind.' Chickens aren't people, but neither are they nothing but hunks of meat. Chickens are chickens, and they deserve to be treated like chickens! This means that we have to give each chicken the space to strut its stuff in front of other chickens.[2]

I like the idea of a "strut-your-stuff" test for human and chicken dignity. If a person doesn't have a chance to strut his or her human stuff in making, growing, and producing a product, then something is wrong. Of course chicken dignity is a different kind of dignity, but it deserves strutting nonetheless.

When we arrived back in town from our initial brainstorming session in Seattle, we were greeted with an invitation to a New Year's Eve party at the home of Dave, the sausage prophet. We had already stepped over the boundary of knowing the names and even being friends with the farmers who were feeding us, but now we were crossing a whole new threshold. We were honored and sort of giddy at the chance to glean information about how to pull off our year of local consumption. At the party, we met one of the farmers

I had spent much of the previous summer trying to lure to the Millwood Market.

Gary Angell is a cowboy-farmer version of Michael Pollan. He's a sustainable farming activist quick with a story about the evils of industrial food practices and tenacious in walking the walk, nurturing a fully integrated sustainable farm on a hardscrabble piece of land called Rocky Ridge Ranch on the western edge of Spokane. Gary's partner on the farm is his wife, So, who grows all the vegetables and greens and operates their booth at farmers' markets. So speaks with a very thick Korean accent, and while I don't always understand her words, she's always ready with a bright smile and a warm hug whenever I stop by her booth at the market.

When we told Gary what we were planning to do he offered that he sells naturally raised processed frozen whole chickens. We were excited to check off a source of protein in our diet as we looked to the coming year. It doesn't take much to get Gary going on the subject of farming and food. Our inquiry about chickens led to a passionate explanation of the evils of industrial farming practices.

He said, "You know most of those industrial chickens, they grow so fast relative to their legs that they can't even stand up. Sometimes their bodies are so huge and their legs so weak that they break their legs when they try to stand up." He lamented that they've genetically modified all the natural instincts out of the birds. He called them "zombie chickens."

I replied, "I've seen signs that describe some poultry as hormone free but then I've also heard that all chickens are hormone free."

Gary explained, "I think those are in reference to growth hormones but I'm more concerned with naturally occurring stress hormones. When chickens are raised packed together in small spaces, the stress they experience causes them to release stress hormones."

It made intuitive sense to me. When we are stressed our bodies release adrenaline and cortisol, so why wouldn't the same kind of mechanisms be at work in stressed-out chickens. The anecdotes were flying, and while the science behind Gary's observations is debatable, his passionate defense of the humane treatment of farm animals was convincing and convicting.

Gary's wife, So, chimed in and insisted, "My chickens are happy chickens. They get to walk around and dig in the dirt. They are happy. Not like those factory chickens." I've never met someone so enthusiastic about the mental health of chickens. And maybe just as chickens release stress hormones when they are under duress, I wondered if the opposite is also true. In the same way we release happy hormones when we feel good, maybe So's chickens have all sorts of good, happy hormones running through their systems. We were going to find out. That first week we stocked up on a couple of frozen whole chickens, one we bought and one So insisted we take as a gift.

While Gary's words of concern about industrial farming practices got our attention and made us wonder if we hadn't been a little disconnected from the animals we eat, our encounter with that first Rocky Ridge Ranch whole chicken showed us just how clueless we were. We thawed it out as instructed, and Nancy, who was fixing up a recipe that required chicken breasts, called me into the kitchen. "Craig can you cut up the chicken for me?"

"Sure, I'd be glad to," I responded as I gathered the cutting board and sharpened the knife.

It wasn't until I put the carcass on the chopping block that it dawned on me that I was thirty nine years old and had never in my life cut up a whole raw chicken. Here's the rundown of my experiences with poultry up until that point:

Carve a Thanksgiving turkey—check,
Tear apart a rotisserie chicken from the grocery store—check,
Assemble the various prechopped up pieces of a chicken on the
    BBQ grill—check,

Cut up a whole raw chicken—insert obnoxious Family Feud buzzer here.

Neither Nancy nor I grew up with chickens, so it's understandable that we'd never gathered eggs from a nest, or chopped the head off a live chicken, or plucked off the feathers or ripped out the guts. In *The Omnivore's Dilemma*, Michael Pollan chronicles his experience slaughtering chickens at Polyface farm. His encounters there evoke a pastoral nostalgia and spark the imagination of a time gone by when we weren't so far removed from the farm. But there was nothing nostalgic about us learning how to cut up a chicken. It was just kind of pathetic.

I sharpened the knife, and as I looked over the bird, I tried to piece together the sections—legs, breasts, and thighs. It was surprisingly difficult to imagine it in a way that resembled what I was looking at. I made one big crunching cut down through the breastbone, dividing the bird in half. The legs were easy to figure out so I lopped them off. It took a little guessing on where to separate the thighs from the rest of the carcass but, sure enough, after five chops we had the chicken parts we were familiar with from trips to the grocery store. Thus began our chicken education.

THE FARMERS NEXT DOOR

There were two wonderful consequences from this experience with the mysterious whole chicken. On the one hand it startled us into recognizing how little we knew about the meat we had eaten for the majority of our lives. We knew it as patties and nuggets and pieces, but our understanding of our animal food system was far from whole. Our cool veneer of being enlightened consumers was laid bare by getting closer to the source of our food.

This experience also confirmed a lesson learned over and over again during the year—hands-on experience in the real world leads to changed behavior. Instead of the red pill in the *Matrix*, it was the whole chicken that started us down a path of dramatic changes in the way we eat animals. I had seen videos about the hideous conditions in factory farms and had read books like *Fast Food Nation: The Dark Side of the All-American Meal* that lifted the veil on industrial food practices. That was all well and good, but it wasn't until I had a whole chicken on the counter and a knife in my hand that we started actually making informed choices about eating meat. And really, it wasn't until after our year was completed and we started housing chickens in the back yard that our eating habits were revolutionized.

In order to explain that journey, I have to step ahead on the trajectory that first whole chicken set us on and describe events beyond December 31, 2008. Fast-forward to early spring 2009. After our year of eating only grass-fed beef from Dave the sausage prophet and eggs and poultry from So the chicken whisperer, we decided to take it to the next level and bring farm animals into our family.

We have had a great relationship with our next-door neighbors who have two children the same ages as ours. We even took down the fence between our homes so the kids could play together on a shared playground set. We were afraid that we might endanger these good relations when we asked them about the possibility of installing a chicken coop within sight of their back porch. To our great surprise they loved the idea and said, "We've been thinking about getting chickens too." By the time we went to pick up our small flock of hens we had five designated "owners." Noel and Jenna (the neighbor girl) got Silver Laced Wyandottes that have a beautiful black-and-white scalloped pattern in their feathers. Lily got a Buff Orpington aptly named Cheesy, after the hen's cheddar-orange feathers. Jacob (the neighbor boy) got Eagle, an Ameracauna chicken that lays green eggs and has a hooked beak like a bird of prey. The last addition to the coop was for Zeina, a neighborhood friend who got a Golden Laced Wyandotte she named Honolulu because she thought "Wyan" sounded like "Hawaiian." Honolulu has beautiful scalloped-pattern feathers of rust and black.

True to form, I hadn't really thought things through before we jumped into chicken ownership. When we brought the fluffy chicks home, they were only a few days old, so we had to figure out where to keep them warm and toasty while they grew hearty enough to go outside in the coop. In retrospect, the garage would have been more than adequate, but for some reason I decided to keep them in the upstairs laundry room in a large makeshift cardboard box next to our bedroom.

We kept them there for four weeks right up until Nancy's parents were due to visit. By then the whole house had a faint barnyard smell to it, and the chickens were occasionally breaking free from their box and mixing with the whites and darks. The day before my in-laws arrived I received an ultimatum from Nancy—either the chickens had to go outside or I had to move into the laundry room with them. In a moment of creative inspiration, I turned our compost bin into a temporary outdoor coop while I finished up the main housing.

Before long the elaborately adorned coop that my friends call the chicken condo was finally completed and we moved our new residents in. The kids were in charge of the sign and decided to dub the coop "Chicken Paradise." Noel assured me that she knew how to spell *Chicken* but she needed help with spelling *Paradise*. In a triumphant moment of completion we hung the colorful sign for the coop that read "Chichen Paradise."

I knew we had entered a new phase of our domestic lives when a friend emailed with a request not long after the coop was completed. She explained that as a teacher she needed to do some field trips to maintain her credential and visits to farms counted toward this requirement. She wondered if it would be okay to visit our house to see our chickens and garden, the implication being that we had arrived at some sort of farm status. I told her that was fine, but warned her that if we were a farm, we had to be one of the most comical varieties around.

For example, one morning I let the chickens out at 6:30 a.m. to range free. They have a rhythm where they roam around and then, two-by-two, take turns laying eggs in the nest. They are usually fairly orderly but on that day all hell broke loose. They clucked and cawed and made a racket because Cheesy, the prima donna of the coop, hogged the nest which drove all the other hens insane. Things settled down and it was time for us to leave and corral the chickens into their coop but Chrysanthemum was missing. We combed the neighborhood yelling, "Chrysanthemum," wondering if chickens recognize their names like dogs.

After twenty minutes of looking we resigned ourselves to losing our first bird. I imagined a hawk swooping down in an instant, leaving no trace, or a giant neighborhood cat or a dog happily heading home with its prize in its mouth. Whatever had happened, she was gone. Suddenly we were a farm under attack, wary of the chicken kidnappers on the loose.

I was headed to the car when Nancy called out that she found the chicken. Turns out Chrysanthemum was sick of the drama of the nest and carved out a nice secluded nesting area under the dense asters alongside the house. Determined to teach her a lesson, I plucked her up with both hands and went to put her in the nest before she could lay the egg. That's what my chicken farmer friends told me to do with renegade layers. Just as I reached for the door of the coop I heard a hard thud by my foot. Chrysanthemum had dropped her egg at my feet like a grenade from four feet up, (or maybe I squeezed it out of her), but in a miracle of oyster shell supplements, the egg didn't break.

But chickens are creatures of habit and after chasing Chrysanthemum around for a couple of days I gave up and let her lay her eggs in the asters. At least we didn't have to post a bunch of "Missing Chicken" posters around the neighborhood.

On another occasion Cheesy, our Buff Orpington, fell ill and just sat in the nest all day. At first I thought she was just broody. That's what my chicken-farmer friend suggested. By the way, I love the word *broody*. Now when I'm feeling cranky and under the weather I use the broody card.

Anyway, Cheesy was more than broody. She started to look sickly, with her comb, the pink tussle of flesh that runs down her head like a Mohawk, turning black. Needless to say I was alarmed when I Googled "black comb chicken" and got a bunch of links to avian flu.

I overcame my fears of the chicken plague and gave Cheesy a chicken physical and discovered that her breast was hard and felt like it was full of gritty silly putty. It turns out she had an impacted crop. Her food was stuck in the first stage of a chicken's digestive system. The girls and I started a regimen of massaging her crop so that the food could pass, and she soon got better. When our neighbor, who thinks our chickens are really spoiled, found out we were massaging the chicken, he nearly impacted his crop from hysterical laughter.

Our status as farmers was further reinforced when we decided to enter the chickens in the Spokane County fair. We had been entering vegetables in the fair for a couple of years. I remember visiting the King County fair near Tacoma as a child, walking through the displays of animals and agriculture, and eating a pile of raspberry-jam smothered scones. But I had no experience as a participant. It was always something other people did, people who lived very different lives from mine.

Entering chickens in the fair took it to a whole new level.

When entry day arrived, we rounded up our brood (it took about forty-five minutes to run them down and box them up) and rolled into the exhibitors parking lot of the fairgrounds, nervous that someone would correctly identify us as being terribly out of place and tell us to go home. We parked our poultry-stuffed station wagon next to all the farm-worn trucks and put our birds in their assigned cages. We got the chickens settled in, said goodbye, and went home. We returned the next day, Friday, for a lesson on how to show the birds for the judges on Saturday.

We showed up Saturday and discovered that Cheesy was on champion's row, boasting best of class and best of breed ribbons. Honolulu won reserve best of breed and best of class. All of our chickens got blue first-place ribbons.

Then it came time for the show. It was easy to just leave the chickens in their cages for the first phase of the judging. It was whole other thing to show them off to a judge. Lily was first up with Cheesy, who was about twice as big as the other chickens on display. (I guess most people get kids small chickens to help them learn to show.) Lily was right next to a girl from the Rux family. We had become familiar with the Rux' from previous visits to the fair where they had dozens of animals on display. All the other kids had cowboy hats and bolo ties. We felt a little like a chicken version of *The Bad News Bears,* and while Lily was clearly outmatched, I took some consolation that if it were a version of cock fighting we would have had the clear advantage.

But this was about knowledge and the craft of displaying chickens, with every other child drawing on experience as part of 4-H or FFA. I had been coaching soccer all morning so I instinctively yelled out instructions to Lily in the middle of the showing, trying to point out the part of the chicken the judge had just asked Lily to identify. The judge gently reprimanded me. I'm not up on chicken-show etiquette, but I'm guessing that heckling the judge isn't okay, so I refrained from any more coaching.

By the end of the week at the fair, after daily visits to clean up the cages and do their required service hours, the girls felt comfortably at home. When they cleaned the cages and carried the birds confidently around the display area, the fair goers who wandered the aisles lit up and asked, "Is that your chicken?" With confidence and pride they responded, "Yes, do you want to pet her?" Kids from these families approached our chickens like they were exotic snakes from South America. These foreign creatures were now part of our household economy, giving us two dozen fresh eggs a week.

I'm not sure when I crossed the line, but one night as Nancy prepared a chicken dinner from a store-bought chicken, I said, "I don't want to eat chicken anymore." I had known for a long time the terrible conditions most meat chickens are raised in—confined in cages, never seeing the light of day even if they are supposedly free-range, living for fourteen miserable weeks on this earth.

"I don't want to eat chicken anymore," I reaffirmed to Nancy.

Somehow having our own chickens, seeing them bathe in the afternoon sun, scratch with glee in the dirt, screech with pride when they lay an egg, and run like big clumsy Weebles had changed my appetite. It took welcoming chickens into our household economy to change my behavior.

MEAT MATTERS

While I had previously expressed a philosophy of opposition to industrial chicken practices, I still went on with my conscience untouched by the occasional chicken sandwich or chicken breast on a salad. But once I had a personal relationship with five chickens, my conscience caught up with my philosophy. My experience trumped my pragmatism. I suspect that one of the reasons the treatment of meat animals in recent years has often had so little dignity is that consumers, like myself, have become far removed from the experiences of these animals. We have exiled farm animals from our living spaces, making it illegal in most residential developments to raise chickens, at least until very recently. For our family, bringing the animals back into our lives helped us realize that the animals are more than just little pieces of meat.

As part of our summer vacation in 2008, we spent a week at a Colorado dude ranch. We had lots of fun riding horses every morning and afternoon but the highlight was spending a day off the trail, rounding up around one hundred yearling cows who were grazing the national forest surrounding the ranch. This high mountain forest had been ravaged by a recent fire, leaving behind a maze of lifeless Ponderosa pines. The wrangler explained that the Forest Service had been expanding the permitted number of cattle allowed to graze in the forest because studies show that managed grazing is beneficial to the regeneration of the land.

We had already made a point of spending time with the people who produce the goods we consume with the intent of becoming more attuned to their hopes, dreams, and challenges. But spending time with the cattle that afternoon served as a precursor of what we would later experience with our chickens.

I found that hanging out with the year-old cows gave me a new respect for them as animals. I will remember their wild eyes, their stubborn disposition, and their desperate sense of being lost when separated from the herd. After spending all day with the animals, I was surprised at my response to being served prime rib for dinner. I felt a new sense of gratitude for the meal. The previously decontextualized pieces of meat had become connected to living, breathing creatures.

My participation in the roundup also cured me of some of my sentimental notions about farm animals. When I started the day, I'd had a mostly pastoral vision for what it is like to rustle cattle. But a couple of hours walking behind a group of smelly, poop covered, not-too-bright animals that had a tendency to mount and hump their fellow travelers was enough to cure me of my idyllic visions. They are worthy of cow dignity, but they are not pets or people. On one end we have a tendency, probably a greater tendency, to commodify and devalue cows, but an absence of experiencing real cows in real places can also lead us to misvalue them.

I'm still up for eating So's happy chickens and Dave's contented cows, but for the most part I'm not as hungry for meat. Our hunger for so much meat is what drives the efficient-but-often-cruel farming practices that bring our meat to market. Meat production, especially beef, is also a major source of greenhouse gases, and the million-gallon moats of manure that result from the CAFOs are environmental disasters waiting to happen. I tend to agree with those advocating that we, in general, eat less meat for our own health and for the health of the environment. In 1970 the average American consumed 40.2 pounds of chicken. In 2007 that number had risen to 86.5 pounds of chicken.[3] Some might argue that this is a sign of progress, but there are plenty of other signs of unhealth in people, the land, and the meat itself that indicate otherwise.

For us, our change in perspective started with simply learning to cut up a chicken, but ultimately it was bringing farm animals into our household economy that transformed our relationship to meat. I like the way lecturer Peter Lennox sums it up in describing his experience with chickens in his backyard:

> If one actually lives with chickens, it's a lot harder to treat them as mere objects. Their preferences are astoundingly obvious, so what possible excuse could there be for giving them any less? If they like greens, why give them pellets? If they like sunbathing, why pack them into a tiny, noisy, smelly place with no natural light? If, as I suspect, the answer is something to do with the 'efficiency' of food production, then the notion of efficiency is horrible, incompetent, brutalised and brutalising, and it's certainly not in the interests of chickens at all.[4]

In cutting up that chicken I began to recognize that our simple world of consumer objects was really a complex interaction between the environment and animals and people, all caught up in a web of practices, some more sustainable and ethical than others.

Not long after the county fair, Lily had to do a "culture basket" presentation in her second-grade class. The students were invited to bring in artifacts from their family life and do a presentation about their family culture. One of Lily's artifacts was the ribbon she won for best of breed chicken. Before she left for school that day, she did a practice run of her presentation. She held up the ribbon and said, "This is our first year of being real-live farmers."

I love the image of our family as farmers even if we do live in the suburbs in a master-planned community. I wonder what it would be like if all of us imagined ourselves as farmers, caretakers and stewards of the land and animals that provide us with food.

IV: Autumn

What I love best in autumn is the way that Nature takes her curtain as the stage folks say. The banners of the marshes furl, droop, and fall. The leaves descend in golden glory. The ripe seeds drop and the fruit is cast aside. And so with slow chords in imperceptible fine modulations the great music draws to its close, and when the silence comes you can scarce distinguish it from the last far-off strains of the woodwinds and the horns.[1]
—Donald Culross Peattie

There is a time for everything,
and a season for every activity under the heavens:
a time to be born and a time to die,
a time to plant and a time to uproot. . . .
I have seen the burden God has laid on the human race.
He has made everything beautiful in its time.
—Eccl. 3:1-2, 10-11

IN A YEAR OF UNLIKELY TWISTS AND TURNS, THE CLOSING of summer brought us to yet another strange but fulfilling accomplishment: Lily and Noel captured the coveted grand champion prize for largest rutabaga at the Spokane County fair.

The fact that ours was the only rutabaga entered that year didn't make the award any less meaningful.

For about one glorious week, our labyrinth vegetable garden looked beautiful. The short teddy bear sunflowers that surrounded our central patch of grass erupted in soft pom-poms of finely textured yellow. An abundance of small orange and large red tomatoes hung on the green vines like Christmas ornaments. The green peppers turned different shades of purple, yellow, and red. (I didn't know that all green peppers if given enough time soaking up the sun eventually turn to vibrant colors.) The tops of the carrots burst through the surface of the soil, bright orange rings topped with fine-leafed ferns. One scoop of the hand in the patch of spuds brought forth perfectly rounded purple Peruvian potatoes. The smooth khaki butternut squash rested under a lush green canopy of leaves. The cedar-pole teepees vanished under the tightly wrapped vines of green beans.

For one week all the hard work, all the planning, all the weeding manifested itself in unadulterated beautiful abundance. But very quickly the synchronicity of the garden collapsed. Powdery mildew enveloped the squash leaves turning them brown and withered. The weight of the jalapeños toppled the pepper plants and the rest of the greenery started to show the yellow of cool autumn nights. The mammoth sunflowers took a bow, pointing their heavy pock-marked faces to the ground, shoulders slumped in exhaustion from faithfully following the movement of the sun day after day. Even the weeds relented, giving up the battle for another year. Just as soon as the garden arrived at a colorful crescendo, it began the inevitable journey back to topsoil brown, back to where it came from.

On the one hand it seems ridiculous to spend more than seven months working tirelessly for one week of soaking up the satisfaction of arriving at our goal. On the other hand it's hard to imagine it any other way. Life is like that, with most of our days spent working toward short-lived fulfillments.

This is one of the things I appreciate most about the church-year calendar, where the emphasis for the majority of the year is on our experience of waiting and anticipating. Both Advent and Lent conclude in ultimate fulfillments, the birth and resurrection of Jesus, but the seasons that precede these days of fulfillment are by design intentional times of waiting.

Autumn is the one natural season without a corresponding big church-year liturgical event. The winter has Advent, spring has Lent, summer has Pentecost, but autumn falls during what the church calls "ordinary time." For a good thirty-three weeks out of the year the Sundays are a relentless march of ordinary time. This is actually a fairly recent naming of the non-Advent and non-Lenten seasons. They used to be labeled by the number of Sundays after Pentecost. So the title for a given Sunday would have been the twenty-second week after Pentecost. In the late 1960s, there was a shift in terminology to call it ordinary time. There is some debate about the meaning of *ordinary*, that perhaps it doesn't mean what it sounds like it means. But I think it's actually an unintentional stroke of genius.

At the heart of the good news of the gospel is that God has chosen to come among the ordinary, to surround the ordinary with holiness. The God who is born under the glorious light of the star walks with us in the flesh. The Jesus who miraculously rises from the dead also joins us in the common experience of death.

Autumn is ordinary time. Following the glorious satisfaction of the harvest, it's time to walk once again in the rhythms of waiting and anticipating, resting in the certainty that spring will come again, grateful for past provision and longing for a distant hope.

CHAPTER 11

Green Christians

"GOING GREEN" WAS NOT HOW WE WOULD HAVE DESCRIBED our plans for the year, but the nature of our rules placed us square in the middle of conversations about sustainability, carbon footprints, reducing waste, recycling, and reusing. By chance, our decision to eat local for a year coincided with a wave of interest in local foods. We suddenly found ourselves engaged in conversations about food miles, GMOs (Genetically Modified Organisms) and CAFOs (Concentrated Animal Feeding Operations). Our decision to cut back to one vehicle and reduce our consumption of fuel placed us in a growing community of people who are biking and walking and intentionally reducing their carbon footprints. When we went to the used clothing store, we were greeted by signs that proclaimed, "Go Green, Buy Used." We had become accidental environmentalists, and as we walked in these communities and conversations as Christians we found ourselves at the meeting place of faith and environment, sometimes in a very public way.

In 2009 our church farmers' market gained some infamy in Washington state when the Department of Revenue revoked the property tax exemption on our parking lot because we were hosting what they categorized as commercial activity. From our little neighborhood market that had to pay $800 in taxes, the dominoes fell as it became apparent that other churches and nonprofit organizations throughout the state were hosting markets in their parking lots, including the University District Market in Seattle, recently dubbed "one of the best" neighborhood farmers' market in America. Suddenly that market faced a $60,000 annual tax bill because it was held at a nonprofit community center.

This led to a statewide effort to change the law so that churches and other nonprofits could host markets without losing their exempt status. In the spring of 2010, the legislation was passed and signed into law. These events caught the attention of a reporter from *The New York Times,* which resulted in an article that included a photo of me standing in our sanctuary with stained glass shimmering in the background under the headline, "Pastors in Northwest Find Focus in 'Green.'" The journalist was interested in how mainline churches that have mostly been in decline might be reengaging their neighborhoods and growing in size by emphasizing "going green," especially in the Pacific Northwest where caring about the environment is a big deal but going to church is not.

I figured that would be the height of the hype, but then a couple days after the article came out, Al Gore highlighted it on his online journal and tweeted the story to his two million plus Twitter followers: "A new trend—Green Pastors." He offered his interpretation of the story online saying, "The environmental and religious communities have long been allies in the fight to save our planet. This trend is increasing in the Northwest where churches are finding environmentalism can help fill their pews."[1]

It was fascinating to me the way our concern for the environment in the church was squeezed into the narrative of turning around declining churches and filling the pews. The *Times* journalist made sure to point out that our membership had grown during the farmers' market era, along with highlighting the comments of an Episcopal priest whose go green efforts did not stop their church from declining in membership. It seemed a strange way to frame our efforts, but that was the narrative that bubbled to the surface—"Going Green" as church marketing strategy.

When the Al Gore tweet went out, I logged onto the @algore search feed, and in a miracle of social networking, I could see in real time that his original message was retweeted about every ten seconds to thousands of other Twitter followers. They added their own comments as they passed on the link. Some were affirming, saying, "Green Pastors—awesome," or "Green Pastors—Praise God," or "Green Pastors—It's about time." Others were less complimentary. They said things like, "Green Pastors—Total Crap." Or "Green Pastors—do they have private jets like you @algore?" One by one the tweets trickled down the computer screen as new responses were added, a modern debate in progress—but one response caught my attention.

Someone wrote, "Churches don't support green efforts until they realize it helps attract new members. #religionisevil."

I lobbed a tweet into the mix pleading that it's not just about getting new members, but the story had already been framed: going green is good for business in churches, it helps fill pews, and might just increase membership rolls.

I wondered after all the dust settled why Al Gore got to have the saving the world story and the church got stuck with the filling-pews story. How did we end up as the cultural mercenaries out to save our churches and the environmentalists were the ones interested in saving the world?

I monitor several newsfeeds and many of them include issues of the environment. So I have grown used to seeing variations on the phrase, "Saving the World," in the headlines of the stories. A Google news search of headlines on any given day might be topped by the question, "Can Bill Gates Save the World?" followed by *Time* article, "A Cost Effective Way to Save the World." The *Wall Street Journal* predictably chimes in with an article "How to Make Money and Save the World." The topper for me was when Whole Foods Market started carrying Save Your World™ personal care products. Notice I had to put the "TM" for trademark in there, because some personal-care-product company has legal rights to the phrase.

On the positive side, there seems to be a tacit agreement that the world needs saving. There is recognition of a world crisis that needs resolving. Amen to that. But the shadow side is the presumption that somehow this saving work is within our grasp, and we can make money and have soft skin while we do it. Instead of really engaging the deep question of salvation, wholeness, and peace in the world, this dialogue suggests we have the whole world in our hands. I would argue that the most hopeful place of responsibility, when it comes to the environment, is to take a more humble view of our place in the world. Karl Barth talked about this when he described theology as the only knowledge-seeking endeavor in which, instead of standing over the microscope looking down through the lens at the object of study, we stand on the stage looking up at God. We are created, not creator and our recognition of that makes all the difference. It opens up the possibility for us to participate in the grand story of God's saving work in the world, which includes decisions about money and even personal-care products but does not presume that these choices give us the power to save the world.

THE GREEN CHURCH

The key phrase in that previous statement might be "participate." During our year, the book *Unchristian: What a New Generation Really Thinks about Christianity . . . and Why It Matters* was creating waves of conversation in the American church. According to a study reported in the book, the actual lifestyle differences between people who identify themselves as "born-again Christians" and those who do not is surprisingly minimal.

The book reports, "We discovered that born-agains were distinct on some religious variables. . . . However, when it came to nonreligious factors—the substance of people's daily choices, actions and attitudes—there were few meaningful gaps between born-again Christians and non-born-agains."[2] The book defines "born-again" as people who say they have "made a personal commitment to Jesus that is still important and that the person believes he or she will go to heaven at death, because that person has confessed his or her sin and accepted Christ as Savior. That's it."[3] This is a fairly broad definition that includes not just conservative Evangelicals, but also progressive Evangelicals and a good portion of mainline Christians and Catholics as well.

The authors emphasize that in every study they have conducted, apart from religious activities, they have failed to find substantial lifestyle differences among born-again Christians and non-Christians. They do go on to offer some examples where born-again Christians show some glimmers of uncommon virtue. The survey responses suggest that born-again Christians are less likely to use profanity in public (26 percent to 38 percent), are less likely to have purchased a lottery ticket (26 percent to 34 percent), and are more likely to have helped someone in poverty (53 percent to 45 percent). But in passing, without comment they also report, "Recycling was less common among born-again Christians (68 percent versus 79 percent)."[4]

When I first read that I was baffled. Why in the world would followers of Jesus be less likely to recycle? It is one thing for Christians to fail to distinguish ourselves but how could it be that we don't recycle as much as the average Joe. What could possibly be working against the cultural norms that would leave us less committed to a hallmark of environmental concern? Was it a demographic or geographic anomaly? Maybe these self-reporting "born-agains" are disproportionately located in parts of the country that have less infrastructure for recycling than average? Or perhaps they are disproportionately representative of older generations that are less likely to recycle. Or maybe there is something terribly wrong with the church in America.

A recent Pew study on religion and American life reinforces the gap between Christians and others when it comes to engagement with environmental issues. The report states:

> Although a majority of every major religious group in the United States supports stricter environmental measures, there are some differences in degree. For instance, only slim majorities of members of evangelical churches (54%) support the imposition of stricter environmental laws. Members of non-Christian faiths, by contrast, are much more likely to believe that stricter environmental regulations are worth the economic costs. More than two-thirds of Jews (77%), Buddhists (75%), Hindus (67%), Muslims (69%), and the unaffiliated (69%) support stricter environmental laws. Further, more than seven in ten atheists (75%), agnostics (78%) and the secular unaffiliated (72%) say stricter environmental laws are worth the cost.[5]

The survey reports that Christians from mainline churches are more likely to support stricter environmental laws (64 percent), which still leaves this group at the low end compared to other religious groups.

I recognize this question about environmental regulations enters the murky waters of American politics, but how can it be that atheists are almost 25 percent more likely to support stricter environmental regulations than evangelical Christians? Is it as simple as partisan politics or is there something more going on here? Does American Christianity somehow have a short circuit when it comes to the environment? As someone who laments these statistics, I wonder not only why Christians are lagging, but why Christians aren't the leaders and exemplars when it comes to caring for God's creation. I'm not disappointed that we're not average. I am disappointed that we're not ahead of the curve in the same way that we are less likely to cuss in public. By all rights the church should be on the cutting edge of environmental concern.

We affirm that God created all things and upon completing the work, proclaimed it all "good." We are the ones who inherit Adam and Eve's commission to take care of the garden. We passionately sing with the psalmist, "The earth is the LORD's and everything in it" (Ps. 24:1). We stand in the tradition of Israel in the Promised Land, where they are told by God, "The land is mine and you reside in my land as foreigners and strangers" (Lev. 25:23). We know all too well our tendencies to abuse and exploit God's good gifts. As Paul says, because of sin, "the whole of creation has been groaning as in the pains of childbirth" (Rom. 8:22). We are the ones who try to get our heads on straight in this mixed-up world by following Jesus' instructions to look at the birds of the air and consider the lilies of the field. We are the ones who carry today the present hope that in Christ all things are held together and the future promise that God is redeeming all things, "making everything new" (Rev. 21:5).

We have a special commission as God's people to care and advocate for the poor and as Christian mission organizations like Plant With Purpose have made clear, we can't advocate for the poor in places like Haiti without addressing deforestation and sustainable agricultural practices. We can't love our neighbor without also caring for the creation that sustains our neighbors with work and food and health. Loving our neighbor is an environmental act.

TURNING THE TIDE

Someone might have a good case for dismissing the significance of the statistics I cite above about Christians being behind the curve on the environment, but the truth is that most Christian leaders, especially in Evangelical circles these days, would acknowledge a failure to lead in this area.

About halfway through our year, Richard Cizik, the vice president for governmental affairs of the National Association of

Evangelicals, was named one of *Time* magazine's one hundred most influential people in the world for his efforts at promoting *creation care*, the preferred term for environmentalism in evangelical circles. While Cizik's efforts in advocacy were noteworthy, his presence on the list was primarily because his efforts represented a new development in American Evangelical Christians willing to ally themselves with the environmental movement.

In October 2006 Bill Moyers chronicled this growing concern for the environment in a documentary where he asked the question, "Is God Green?" While mainline Protestant churches had been affirming God's concern for the planet for the better part of a century, Evangelicals had long been suspicious of the green movement. The reasons for this opposition are multifaceted, including a theological emphasis on the holiness of God, a hangover from wrangling with what were perceived as godless radicals in the 1960s, and in more recent years the blurring of lines between conservative American politics and the American church. We all know the routine. It's the spotted-owl opportunist vs. the chainsaw-wielding logger, the oil baron vs. the tree-hugging activist, the Birkenstock vs. the steel-toed work boot. The issue is overrun with caricatures, so no wonder many churches have been less than eager to jump in.

Cizik's work on the issue of global warming was not without controversy, but all indications seem to be that the tide has turned. Driven largely by passionate young adults, conversations about the environment are now taking place in churches across the country. Given the newly emerging openness to going green in the church, I want to offer my humble perspective on the opportunity of this moment.

Like Al Gore and the *New York Times* journalist, many people have commended our family's efforts at sustainable living as good promotional fodder for the church. These efforts have led to greater visibility for the church in the community and more visitors on Sunday mornings. But I have to agree with my Twitter antagonist that if a church's efforts at going green are nothing more than window dressing to attract socially conscious church shoppers, then these efforts are misguided. I wouldn't go so far as to call them evil, but they are certainly reflections of a larger problem that leads people to see religion as shallow and manipulative. It's the kind of thing that has led to the "nones"—people who claim no religious affiliation—becoming the fastest growing religious group in America.

Instead of dismissing the current laggard status of the church when it comes to environmental concerns, I think it's helpful to amplify it. The statistics will shift quickly, and the average Christian will fall into line with norms around recycling and going green. But before that happens there is a golden opportunity to consider what this little cultural fault line reveals. In my opinion it points to both a core crisis in the contemporary church—the disconnect between our conception of the spiritual and the material—and an incredible opportunity to not just embrace green bags and composting, but to embrace the incarnation of Jesus as the model for the life of the church.

GOING GREEN AS INCARNATION

I approach current conversations around the church in North America through the lens of what has become known as the missional church movement, especially as the word *missional* is defined in Darrel Guder and Lois Barrett's book, *Missional Church: A Vision for the Sending of the Church in North America*, and the writings and thoughts of Lesslie Newbigin. The emergent or emerging church is a higher profile but similar stream of recent conversation about the challenges facing the church in a postmodern world. I think of the missional-church movement as the preppy, mainstream brother-in-law of the emergent church—less comfortable with tattoos and body piercings. Or maybe it's the boring Windows PC of postmodern engagement to the emergent church's much hipper Mac.

I guess it tells you something about me that I'm most comfortable in missional circles.

For the last seven years I have been enrolled in Fuller Theological Seminary's Missional Leadership Doctor of Ministry cohort. It's taken me so long to complete my degree that during that time I've seen the word *missional* run the full cycle of being new and revolutionary, to being very popular and mainstream, to now being overused to the point of it being nearly meaningless. Despite this inevitable progression, there is a distinctive perspective in the missional-church conversation that is especially relevant to a church that is making the turn toward environmental concerns. Alan Roxburgh, a Canadian pastor and theologian and one of my instructors in the D.Min. program, has identified this missional distinctive more clearly than most.

In his book, *The Missional Leader: Equipping Your Church to Reach a Changing World*, Roxburgh makes a distinction between the modern concept of extraordinary enlightenment and a missional imagination that grows up out of the ordinariness of the people in the church. He points to the incarnation of Jesus as the core theological framework for understanding this distinction. He says, "Jesus' birth stories tell us that God and God's future meet us—in the ordinary and everyday." He explains that modern instincts that divide the spiritual and material have led the church to "dematerialize and spiritualize Jesus, limiting God's engagement to some inner, spiritual experience that is disembodied from most of the public and material engagement of the world." If this modern philosophical virus has indeed infected our churches, than it's no wonder Christians recycle less than most. If the spiritual and material realms of the world are seen as distinct kingdoms that don't intersect, it's not surprising that concern for the environment is considered peripheral to the work of God.

I agree with Roxburgh that the answer to this disconnect is not for the church to participate in the material realm only in so much as it gets people interested in the spiritual. Such an approach leaves the assumption firmly in place that this divide is irreconcilable. For a church that finds itself trapped in these dualisms, the answer is found in the incarnation of Jesus. Roxburgh says,

> We come perilously close to losing the recognition held by the early church that the Incarnation not only changes everything but becomes the center from which all reality must now be understood and all of life practiced. In the Incarnation, God meets us in the concreteness of our place and time.

The good news of the gospel is that God comes into the world not just as a spiritual being, but that God comes embodied in the flesh, spirit, and material wedded in an inseparable unity. Any honest engagement with the person of Jesus disrupts efforts to imagine a world neatly divided between the spiritual and material.

Earlier in the book I mentioned Paul's description in Colossians 1 about all things being redeemed in Christ. A companion to that verse is found in Ephesians 1, where Paul writes,

> In him we have redemption through his blood, the forgiveness of sins, in accordance with the riches of God's grace that he lavished on us. With all wisdom and understanding, he made known to us the mystery of his will according to his good pleasure, which he purposed in Christ, to be put into effect when the times reach their fulfillment—to bring unity to all things in heaven and on earth under Christ. (1:7-10)

Jesus comes, not to reinforce spiritual and material divisions but to bring all things under the banner of God's love and justice. In a great irony, the key to a down-to-earth faith is an abiding reflection on the cosmic Christ. The newly discovered openness in the church toward concern for the environment is best understood in light of this. It is as an opportunity for the church to rediscover and renew our place in the grand story of God's redeeming work in Jesus Christ, God's kingdom coming on earth as it is in heaven.

It's also an opportunity to save ourselves from the small, petty story of filling pews. When I think about the church today, I'm reminded of an account I once read about John Muir. A wilderness explorer and pioneer of America's national parks, Muir evidently had a habit of going out into the woods and climbing trees during ferocious storms, exulting in the wildness of the experience. On one occasion, when he returned from such a venture "wet as a muskrat and dripping puddles," his hosts

> bestirred themselves for his comfort, pitying him for having been in such frightful weather. But with face glowing as if he has just come down from Mount Sinai, he exclaimed, "Don't pity me. Pity yourselves. You stay here at home, dry and defrauded of all the glory I have seen. Your souls starve in the midst of abundance!"[5]

Too often those of us in the church are starving in the midst of the abundant scope of what God is up to in the world. While environmentalists are setting a course to save the world, the church debates whether more padding in the pews and more electric guitar will compel Sunday-morning prospects to return. It's "How do we save the church?" not "How do we save the world?" "Dry and defrauded" is not a bad way to describe the confines of these conversations. Seriously engaging issues of environmental concern forces the church to admit that God is up to something in the world beyond the confines of church programs and facilities.

MOVING INTO THE NEIGHBORHOOD

While the missional church conversation is full of complex theory and analysis, I am indebted to Alan Roxburgh for a bit of advice that captures the heart of what I'm trying to say here. One of the years of study in the missional leadership program focused on entering the community around our congregations. After a week's worth of discussion and philosophical inquiry, Roxburgh summed it all up by saying to a room full of pastors, "Get your butt out of your office." My pastoral colleagues and I all giggled at the invitation. Like a child whose parents just found the stash of Halloween candy hidden under her bed, we all knew we were guilty of spending the majority of our time holed up in our offices. We recognized that we were more likely to pay a company in a far off place thousands of dollars for a demographic study of our neighbors than we were to go knock on their doors and simply talk to them. His invitation challenged the ways we had divided up the world into sacred and secular, spiritual and material, church and neighborhood.

Roxburgh's convicting challenge is part of the story of this book. His invitation shaped many of the instincts that led our church to start a farmers' market and to our family having new eyes for seeing the work of God unfolding in our neighborhood and community. It also inevitably led to a new attentiveness to the material realities of our lives, turning our family into accidental environmentalists. As Nancy and I asked questions about loving our neighbors we couldn't help but pay attention to issues of land and economics, carbon footprints and farming methods. As we began to consider the far-reaching implications of the incarnation of Christ, it was natural to expect God to be at work in the midst of our middle-class materialisms.

I think that invitation to move out into the neighborhood is a helpful way of thinking about churches taking up concern for the environment. Instead of starting with global issues and controversial debates, it's better to start by simply paying attention to one's neighborhood and community, asking, "What is God up to in this place?" Whether that "place" is farmland or inner-city abandoned lots, an instinct of attentiveness to a local community will inevitably lead us to an incarnational encounter with the environment.

CHAPTER 12

Thailand and Global Economics

Some time in November of 2008, I learned there was a group of people in San Francisco who had also made this their year of deprivation. They called it "The Compact" and their rules were to barter, borrow, or buy secondhand for a year—food, drink, health, and safety necessities excluded. As I read about The Compact, I considered how our rules had worked out for us. And honestly, for making them up over dinner, they held up very well. It helped that our imaginations had been captured by the food piece of our arrangement—we were having a lot of fun with our suburban farm. And our decision to focus on local and Thai goods gave us a little more flexibility than the Compacters.

Still, there were a few places of discontent. We learned you can't buy a used windshield for your car. Used shoes are problematic for nine-year-old girls. But finding satisfactory shoes was a problem before we started out so I'm not quite sure how to gauge that one. We learned that some of the things from Internet sites like eBay and Amazon are presented as used but seem to be new—Craigslist is a more reliable way to acquire truly used stuff. The bottom line is that we purchased a lot less stuff than in the past. It's not like we found a used counterpart to everything we would have purchased in a normal year. When barriers to consumption are in place, it leads to less consumption. We learned that in January, and it still held true by December.

THE LAST LEG

December brought with it the surreal realization that in just a few weeks we would complete our year-long experiment and would soon be riding elephants in the jungles of northern Thailand and careening through the crowded urban streets of Bangkok in a three-wheel Tuk Tuk. Our intensely local journey was about to go global.

Just weeks before our December 25 departure date, we began hearing reports of political unrest that had closed the airport we were due to fly into. To make it all even more nerve-racking, Spokane was experiencing the highest accumulation of snow ever recorded. Our driveway was piled so high with snow it looked like a ski resort parking lot.

The excitement of the impending trip had carried us through the dark days of October and November when our rules felt more like a cruel joke than a constructive exercise. My socks were full of holes, toes protruding like little hernias. The razor blade I had nursed through a whole year was pulling out as many hairs on my face as it was cutting. The summer bounty of fresh vegetables had abandoned us, and once again our diet was drifting back to potatoes and lentils. Nancy was sneaking around, occasionally buying things like mayonnaise and yogurt that I confiscated like a fastidious customs agent, indignant that she would give up so close to the end. We were heading for *Lord of the Flies* territory when the reality of going to Thailand came into view and pulled us out of our malaise. Just when we feared we would limp to the finish, we perked up with excitement and realized we would make it, holey socks be damned. It also helped that I found out Nikon DSLR cameras are made in Thailand. For the first time in a year, my lust for new technology found a mate.

The plan all along had been to wrap up our Christmas Eve worship services at 9 P.M., then drive overnight, a five-hour trek in the best of conditions, to make our noon flight out of Seattle Tacoma Airport. With all the heavy snow, the mountain pass that delivers folks from eastern Washington to western Washington had been closed for most of the week leading up to Christmas. But through a complex series of precisely timed maneuvers reminiscent of the Lewis and Clark expedition, we walked through the doors of a Korean Air flight in Seattle on Christmas Day and landed twenty-four hours later at Suvarnabhumi Airport on the outskirts of Bangkok. With Thai products and foods approved as part of our consumption plan, we had essentially made it to the end. Our precarious balancing act was over. But in some ways our adventure was just kicking into high gear.

We were greeted at the airport by more than a dozen of Nancy's friends from the Christian school in central Bangkok. Their friendships had been forged across a cultural divide years before, so even though it had been ten years since Nancy's last visit, it was an epic reunion with everyone speaking in high-pitched Thai exclamations of joy. These friends had taught Nancy how to speak the language, and how to walk through the house with gentle feet instead of heavy American feet, and how to cook with unusual Thai ingredients like fish sauce and kiefer lime leaves. She was delighted to see them, and the feeling was mutual.

As our van sped through the midnight streets of Bangkok and Nancy and her friends filled the car with indecipherable conversation, I sat with a stunned sense of gratitude. In a fluke of time zones, it was now late into the evening of December 27. It had been exactly a year since Nancy and I started asking restless questions about the state of our lives. We started this adventure in a Thai restaurant in a nondescript strip mall in Renton, Washington, and we were now driving through the streets of Thailand speeding past strip malls full of Thai restaurants, which to my surprise were throbbing with activity in the middle of the night.

When we arrived at our dormitory room at the school, we were greeted by festive posters with pictures of Nancy that welcomed us with written greetings: "Good memorize with Nancy," and "We glad Nancy here." There was even a poster with a picture of me and the girls under the heading, "Yeh! Nice to meet Good-win family."

"Yeh!" was a good way to describe how we felt as we awoke the next morning to the smells of Thai food cooking in the school's outdoor cafeteria. After a year of eating local, our first full day in Thailand fittingly revolved around food. All morning the women worked in the kitchen preparing a meal in honor of our arrival. It was such a feast we felt like foreign dignitaries welcomed with a state dinner.

Later in the day we went about an hour south of Bangkok near Nakorn Prathom to a riverside market, a football-field-sized maze of food vendors, the Millwood Farmers' Market times one hundred. We were the only "farang," or "white people," in the huge crowd roaming the skinny aisles.

The food items looked like creatures from a Guillermo Del Toro movie: huge melons called jack fruit with infinite unfolding pieces of yellow flesh inside, spikey football-sized fruits called durian, full of pillowy sections that taste like garlic-flavored marshmallows. Their odor is so pungent that the trains have signs picturing durian with a prohibitive red X over them. Smoking was okay, but no durian please. The purple and green mangosteens had such pure colors they looked like vivid cartoon illustrations. Baskets were heaping with golfball-sized rambotan, whose bright red bodies are covered in thick neon green hairs. There were mangos, papayas, star apples , longan, lychee, guava, custard apples, and pineapple. Fresh salad greens were on display, housed in clear plastic bags inflated like balloons, steamy vegetable terrariums. The air was filled with the smells of steaming fried fish, roasted duck, pickled bamboo shoots, and smoldering charcoal. A blind beggar walked the center of the crowded aisles singing karaoke style into a microphone attached to a personal PA system hanging from her neck. The merchants yelled out the virtues of their whole roasted ducks with the cadence of an energetic auctioneer. My orderly antiseptic American senses were overwhelmed and exhilarated.

Oh to be a locavore in tropical Thailand.

Noel and Lily walked arm in arm with the some of the children from the school who came with us to the market. Their eyes were wide with curiosity and just a glimmer of anxiety. Everywhere they turned, they faced a steep learning curve, from going to the bathroom by squatting instead of sitting, to holding back from petting the packs of stray dogs that roamed the streets. They breathed a sigh of relief and relaxed when we found a vendor selling ice cream cones.

We couldn't get into the market without walking by a series of shimmering Buddhist temples, including one that was guarded at its stairway entrance by a ten-foot-high fiberglass leghorn chicken. After our experience discovering connections between faith and chickens, I couldn't help but chuckle. The spirit/material dualism that is so common in the Western world was nowhere to be seen. Monks with their bright orange smocks mingled with the crowd in the glorious materiality of the market scene.

Our whole day was lived around the traditions and sensuousness of food. It was a day of community and connection, not unlike what we had experienced during our year in Spokane, but instead of an experiment at the margins of the consumer culture, it was an encounter with a way of life at the center. Wherever we went in Bangkok, life was mediated through food, one street corner at a time.

When we met friends at the Chinese Presbyterian Church the next day to attend worship, our first order of business was stopping by a rustic noodle shop for my first ever 9 A.M. dose of fish ball soup. We were told the restaurant had been in operation for eighty years. After worship we had lunch and stopped by a street vendor for a banana pastry fried in a giant wok as crowds of people passed by.

You might think it's not all that extraordinary to eat breakfast and lunch and follow it up with something sweet, but there was something different going on here.

Our experience with food in Bangkok reminds me of how a pastor friend from Brazil, Claudio Oliver, helped me understand two unique words used to talk about food in Latin America. He explained to me that "*alimento* is what nutritionists recommend for you; *comida* is what your mum makes for you. *Comida* is what you would call soul food: family together, people talking, warm fresh veggies, sweet potatoes, corn bread, laughing, crying, prayer, thanksgiving, culture, old history, little ones learning who we are through food."

Our first days in Thailand had been an experience of this kind of soul food, discovering and confirming our connections with others, tasting and seeing that the Lord is good, finding in the chicken—among other things—sustenance for our souls. Our year of wandering markets in Spokane had in many ways been a lesson discovering *comida* in an *alimento* culture.

Dubble Bubble Diplomats

We planned our trip in stages. We'd spend the first couple of days in Bangkok at the Christian school and then travel north to Chiang Mai where we would stay with missionary friends for a couple of days. From there we'd travel northeast to stay with a pastor friend who runs an orphanage in Chiang Rai, a stone's throw from the famous Golden Triangle where Thailand, Laos, and Burma all converge. If everything worked out we'd stop and visit with the folks from the Upland Holistic Development Project (UHDP), an organization that works with indigenous tribes in northern Thailand.

In July of 2008, we decided to use $600 of our economic stimulus check to make microloans and/or donations to villagers in Thailand through an organization called Plant With Purpose which is working with the UHDP. UHDP is a Christian nonprofit that seeks to enact their faith in earthy ways, including helping impoverished hill-tribe people with the reforestation of depleted land, gaining access to clean water, building microenterprise, and assisting refugees with acquiring all the important citizenship papers.

Our time in Chiang Mai was delightful. Our first full day included riding elephants, petting tigers, and culminated in the whole family getting Thai massages while dressed in distinctive pink pajamas. I fell in love with mangos, sticky rice smothered in sweetened condensed milk, and Ko Soi, a northern Thai soup specialty.

On New Year's Eve we got on a bus and headed north to meet up with Tui, one of the directors for UHDP. While we were waiting for our departure, Nancy stepped off the bus for a few minutes, and I mistakenly refused to give her seat to a Buddhist monk who seemed unusually insistent that he be allowed to join me in the seat. I successfully fended him off only to find out when Nancy returned that you never refuse the monks. They are everyday celebrities in Thai culture, and apparently they get their pick of bus seats. I was further mortified when I realized that we'd be sitting three to a seat and not two to a seat. This was the one time I was glad not to understand the conversation going on around me.

People seemed a little surprised and confused when we told them where we wanted to be let off the bus. No one else got off as we carted our luggage to an empty dirt parking lot in the middle of nowhere to wait for a man we'd never met. Thankfully Tui pulled up in his Toyota four-by-four just as the bus pulled away. Because this was the least confirmed part of our trip, we had fairly low expectations. We thought we'd just drive through a couple villages and get a tourist's perspective of the area. We had no idea that we'd end up right in the middle of UHDP's work.

We drove on a rut-filled dirt road for about ten miles, passing elephants, crossing creeks, and adding new scars to the bottom of Tui's truck. On the way he explained that the village we were going to was made up of about one hundred displaced people, mostly Palaung refugees from across the border in Burma. Their people had been victims of the notorious Burmese army who had driven them from their homeland, often laying land mines in the surrounding forest to keep them from returning home to support the resistance. The Palaung endured forced labor, rape, and all kinds of unspeakable injustice at the hands of the military. Most of them have no citizenship in Thailand and no official claim to the land they inhabit.

Tui told us about the exploitation of the hill tribes by adventure-travel outfits that arrange for wealthy Westerners to visit and even sleep in the villages. As he explained, this could be a good opportunity for the villagers, but the locally owned agencies typically charge the guests large amounts of money but give the village less than a dollar per person for a visit.

Tui explained and even lamented a little that in their work with Palaung people, who are Buddhist and animist, UHDP is unable to overtly proclaim their Christian faith. This is apparently a condition of their presence in the village. They do all of this work without speaking the name of Jesus, although I'm sure it is common knowledge that Tui and his coworkers are Christians. It's never hard for the 98 percent to identify the 2 percent.

It was inspiring to see their faith lived out in such significant ways within these confines. In my experience of the American church, we are too often content that the mission is accomplished when we say the word "Jesus." We take St. Francis's counsel, "Proclaim the gospel and when necessary use words," and turn it around to say, "Proclaim the gospel and when necessary use actions." It was refreshing to see that at least in one village in the middle of nowhere, there is a vital witness to an integrated, whole kingdom of God, where citizenship papers on earth are not irrelevant to citizenship papers in heaven.

We pulled into a village of two dozen bamboo structures with lush green hillsides rising up around us. I was feeling a bit self-conscious as the villagers in traditional bright red-and-black-patterned dress peered in our direction. I feared we would be seen as just another group of *farang* coming to look at the exotic people, take pictures, and exploit them in one way or another.

Still not sure what we were going to do in the village, we followed Tui as he greeted the villagers and motioned for us to go with him.

"Where are we going Tui?" I asked.

"I'm going to take you to the head man's house. Hopefully he's there and we can have a talk." Every Palaung village has a head man who is elected as the equivalent of a mayor of the village. We were apparently going to the mayor's mansion.

We arrived at the largest bamboo hut in the village, which was sitting up off the ground on wood piers like a beach house. We took off our shoes and left them at the foot of the stairway with a pile of other shoes and flip flops that adorned the landing. We followed Tui up to the porch and stepped into the awkward silence of an open, dark room with filtered light crisscrossing the dusty air like dull spotlights shining in from the midday sun. About a dozen people lounged on colorful bamboo mats that covered the floor. The head man sat directly across from us, legs folded, wearing a black satin jacket with a tattered badge sewn over the right breast with the words "New York Constable." He seemed young to be the head man. He had a thin face, a dark shock of tussled hair, and jaw that never unclenched. He stared off into the distance as Tui introduced us.

We joined the others on the floor, sitting cross-legged, and listened in on the conversation, with Tui translating bits and pieces of the dialogue. I was thrilled to enter into the village's life in such an intimate way, but it presented a particularly challenging parenting moment. Our girls were in that stage of development where they found it hard to sit still for more than a minute, let alone sitting cross-legged on a bamboo mat. They had also recently been practicing the multiplicity of ways you can apply the word "boring" to any given situation. After ten minutes of sitting I was starting to see signs of impending squirms and whiny protests. I did my best to make it known to the girls by the look on my face that they had better sit quietly like little angels or they were going to feel the wrath of the head man of the Goodwin household. When not negotiating with the girls, I looked for as yet unconfirmed signs on the faces of our hosts that we were welcome guests.

In one corner of the room a teenager sat in front of a small card table, a twenty-year-old TV with a homemade set of rabbit ears on the shelf behind him. A woman and her baby sat next to the table. The woman handed the young man a small plastic bag filled with crumpled Thai paper money and coins. At some point it dawned on me that this was the bank, and the woman was depositing money and making payments on her loan as part of the microloan program to which we had contributed. Our tax stimulus payment made the unlikely journey from our bank in Millwood, Washington, to a well-worn baggie in the jungles of northern Thailand.

Tui pointed to the transaction and then gestured to us as he explained to the head man in a Palaung dialect that we had donated money to the microloan program. I thought this might elicit a smile or bridge the gap we were sensing but the head man responded simply by saying that he would like to provide us with a receipt. We explained that this was not necessary, but he insisted and in a gesture of gratitude he motioned for his right-hand man to pour us all a glass of water.

From the time we got a half dozen shots for the worst sounding diseases known to man at the district health office in Spokane, to the interactions with almost every one of our Thai hosts, we had been told not to drink the water. All of those foreboding warnings raced through my mind as our host placed a glass of water in front of every member of our family. I had a feeling it would be major sign of disrespect if we didn't accept their offer of a gift, so I smiled and thanked the constable even as Nancy and I whispered to Noel and Lily not to drink it. It seemed that our short-lived career as tribal diplomats in northern Thailand would come to an unfortunate end. We sat smiling, with the water sitting in front of us in a kind of cultural stalemate until Lily, in her fidgety restlessness, kicked her leg out and accidentally knocked over her glass of water, splashing its contents far and wide over the floor of the hut.

As we cleaned up the water, Nancy remembered that we had eight hundred pieces of Dubble Bubble Bubble Gum in the car and thought this might be a good time to share. We intended to give them all to the orphanage in Chiang Rai, but we had enough for ten orphanages. The girls and I went out to the car and grabbed a large bag of the hunks of pink sugar wrapped in blue and pink wax paper. On the way back to the head man's house, we handed out gum to all the kids in the village. Mothers emerged from their huts to make sure their child received as much as the other kids, and also to make sure they got a piece. One woman whose entire mouth was tar black from a lifetime of chewing on betel leaves grabbed a piece of gum, eager to try this American chewing pastime.

We climbed back into the head man's cottage where indifferent looks still prevailed all around. Without prompting, Lily boldly stepped into the socially awkward space and handed all of the serious looking men hunks of gum. One by one they popped the pink cubes in their mouths and started chewing like it was some important American custom of peacemaking. In a few moments the small dark room was filled with the smacking and slurping of fresh Dubble Bubble, and for the first time the head man smiled. Our bubble gum diplomacy worked and thankfully led to a relaxed afternoon in the village learning about the people. The more we learned, the more the hardened looks on their faces made sense.

We discovered that the children of the village had to walk fifteen miles each way to attend the government-run schools, leaving on their trek long before the sun rises in order to get there on time.

Our efforts walking downhill one mile to Pasadena Park Elementary were put in proper perspective.

As we walked the village we noticed that instead of cars in the driveway they had working elephants tied to posts. This made living with one car for a year seem like a luxury reserved for the wealthiest people in the world, which it is.

We observed the neat fenced gardens in the front yards of the huts lined with straw mulch, a technique UHDP was teaching the refugees in order to control weeds without using toxic chemicals. Tearing out our suburban lawn didn't seem quite so subversive in light of the necessities of life among these people.

It wasn't until I noticed a girl in the village wearing a Delta Delta Delta sorority shirt that I realized most of the Western world clothes that adorned the Palaung kids and adults were used discards from America's consumption whirlwind. The black satin jacket with the constable badge worn by the head man had likely found its way into a container of used clothes from a relief agency in the United States. Our experience of buying used clothes by choice was luxurious and abundant in comparison.

I had gone into this expecting to be the observer, but by the time we left I had a sense that we were the ones who had been observed. The villagers had initially seemed like the strange and exotic people, but their poverty, which is the common experience of the majority of the world's population, revealed us as the strange and exotic breed of American consumers who travel with a year's supply of bubble gum and in one afternoon can afford to spend the equivalent of six months of Palaung wages on handmade crafts. It's the kind of close encounter that leaves you feeling you will never be the same again.

As we drove back out the winding road I was reminded of one of the Bible passages we posted on our blog at the beginning of the year:

Our desire is not that others might be relieved while you are hard pressed, but that there might be equality. At the present time your plenty will supply what they need, so that in turn their plenty will supply what you need. Then there will be equality, as it is written: "The one who gathered much did not have too much, and the one who gathered little did not have too little." (2 Corinthians 8:13-15)

We had seen firsthand the powerful impact of our decision to give out of our plenty to those who are hard pressed. But it also drove home how small our contribution was relative to the challenges and needs facing the Palaung. The stark truth is that we had too much, and they had too little. There was little equity in the ways our fortunes had fallen in the world.

It was the last official day of our experiment. We started the year decrying the injustices facing farmers in our backyard and now a full 365 days later we found ourselves in disbelief at the injustices facing the Palaung. Our commitment to live a consumer life with eyes wide open to caring for people above all other priorities had led us on a labyrinthine journey not unlike our garden maze. We wound back and forth not always sure we were heading in the right direction, certain at times we had gone off the track, but sure enough, this last day had the feel of arriving at the center. Our passionate pursuit of the everyday realities of our local lives in Spokane had opened us up to the world. By paying attention to the hopes and dreams of the people in our hometown, we had nurtured an attentiveness and compassion that opened us up to a people not all that different from us who lived half a world away. Despite the vast disparities of our lives, we all chew bubble gum the same way, smacking and slurping and smiling at our common humanity.

CHAPTER 13

A New Year

Every 3 minutes a woman is beaten,
every five minutes
a woman is raped/ every ten minutes
a lil girl is molested . . .
every 3 minutes
every 5 minutes
every 10 minutes
every day.[1]
—"With No Immediate Cause" by Ntozake Shange

Tui dropped us off in Tathon, a small city on the shores of the Mekok River, just one hillside south of the Burmese border. The next morning we awoke to a new year by taking a three-hour boat ride up the river to Chiang Rai. It was a real life IMAX experience, flying through narrow pristine jungle canyons. The drone of the engine, a souped-up weed whacker with a propeller attached to the end, filled the air as we glided past water buffalo and elephants. We arrived in Chiang Rai and were greeted by Rev. Dr. Sirirat Pusurinkham.

Sirirat is a petite woman in her midforties. She has long black hair and a distinguished demeanor. In a male dominated culture, Sirirat exudes strength and confidence. We got to know Sirirat's story from a visit she made to our church a year before when she talked about her work with HIV-positive women and the orphans they left behind.

THE ENDLESS RESCUE

Sirirat grew up in rural Chiang Rai near the Golden Triangle, a hotbed of drug and sex trafficking. By the age of nine, she had watched many friends from her village be sold off by their families to the sex trade in Bangkok.

She says,

> I was so angry and asked many people if they could help. No one would. Three friends were sent to Bangkok to work in the sex trade and people pretended nothing happened. They closed their eyes, their ears, and their mouths to the entire situation. I have kept those friends in my heart, knowing I needed to do something to help children in similar situations.[2]

Sirirat's vision for a Christian response to human trafficking took her to seminary where she penned a dissertation titled, "Child Prostitution in Thailand: A Challenge to the World Christian Community." She has spoken out against human trafficking from her pulpit as pastor of the Presbyterian Church in Chiang Rai and on the floor of the United Nations. I describe her to friends as the Presbyterian Mother Theresa.

Sirirat's work against trafficking evolved in unexpected ways as her friends from school started showing back up in the city of their birth, now carrying with them diseases, especially HIV/AIDS. She watched the women die from these diseases, leaving a generation of motherless children. She also saw how the survivors—the women who live with HIV/AIDS—are marginalized by the community due to fear of the disease. It was stigma on top of tragic stigma.

In response, Sirirat began working with the women to teach them basic craft techniques like sewing and crocheting, so they could take pride in something and occupy their days in exile with something productive. She also began to gather together the lost children, eventually forming an orphanage with more than thirty girls. When we arrived, she was just beginning to make a place for some of the boys. In living out her faith, she made a commitment to ensure these girls didn't end up victim to the same cruel system that destroyed their mothers.

Because of her close encounters with the horrors of the Thai sex trade, Sirirat doesn't hesitate to speak openly and honestly about the ways it dehumanizes and devastates young girls. She is quick with statistics: There are as many as eight hundred thousand girls younger than sixteen years old who are held in some form of enslavement in Thailand. The financial footprint of sex tourism in the country exceeds that of the drug trade or weapons sales. The girls, some as young as ten years old, typically have sex with ten to fifteen men every day, and sometimes as many as twenty to thirty. AIDS is now the leading cause of death in Thailand, with over three-quarters of a million people living with HIV/AIDS.

It's often girls from poor families on the edge of survival that are sold to make money. Villages like the Palaung tribe we visited are especially vulnerable because of the lack of citizenship papers. Many families send their daughters off in good faith believing the promises of unscrupulous people who betray the parents' best intentions to make a better life and the children's best instincts to honor their parents, only to lure the girls into prostitution. It was shocking to hear Sirirat say that they actually discourage relatives from being part of the orphan's lives because there is a risk that if the orphanage lets the girls leave to spend time with aunts and uncles the girls will be sold off or made into house slaves.

As easy as it is for Sirirat to rattle off the numbers and describe the crisis, she just as easily expresses the ways that her faith in Jesus intersects with these real-world circumstances. She describes Jesus' example of caring for the least in our midst. In a complex Thai culture that, for a whole variety of reasons, turns a blind eye to the problem, Sirirat lifts up the church as the entity that should be the exception, shining a bright light of justice on the terrible human cost of the sex industry, working for the liberation of the most vulnerable.

THE COMMON BOND

Our first day at the orphanage culminated in a big birthday cake celebrating the birthdays of all the children. Because of their circumstances, the actual birth date for many of the kids is unknown, so they celebrate everyone's birthday on January 1. There were big smiles all around as we sang and feasted on the cake a local baker donated for the occasion.

After overcoming some initial shyness and despite the language barrier, Noel and Lily quickly became fast friends with the community of children, playing games and connecting with smiles, giggles, and drawings that need no translation. By the third and final day of our stay, our girls had become inseparable from the group of orphans, walking hand in hand, sitting side by side watching Thai soap operas at the ice cream shop, delighted and fascinated by the strange but familiar other. Just as we'd found common ground in chewing bubble gum with the Palaung, I found myself connecting with these girls as a father. I could see how they were thriving in the safety and loving discipline of Sirirat's care and it was hard to fathom what would likely have become of them if they had not been taken in by the church.

It's one thing to imagine anonymous girls being exploited a world away but to live in the midst of these vulnerable children, and see them alongside my own children, opened my heart up in new ways. Just as they began to interact with Noel and Lily as sisters, I couldn't help but drift into thinking of them as daughters and lamenting the way that so many like them are treated as objects to be exploited and consumed just a few hours to the south in the back alleys of Bangkok.

Sirirat put words to what I was feeling. She said, "The problem with the sex trade in Thailand is that the basic nature of human relationship between two human beings is debased to profit making. It is a fundamental violation of the will of God." This observation clarified for me not only what was going on in Thailand but also spoke to what we had been learning back home.

After a bidding farewell to our friends in Chiang Rai, we took a bus back to Chiang Mai, which led to an overnight bus ride to Bangkok, a short flight to Krabi, and a long boat ride to Railey Beach on the southeast coast of Thailand. Railey Beach could only be accessed by long boat, guarded on either side by towering limestone cliffs and it was just a few coves away from James Bond Island with its famous rock formation, Ko Tapu.

Honestly, we had such amazing encounters and serendipities on our trip that the idea of being pampered at a resort didn't hold the allure we thought it might when we originally made our plans. We were tired from the fast pace of our travels and in a bit of shock from having encountered so many people in great need. It was confusing to be suddenly surrounded by sunburned European tourists and greeted in our glamorous resort room with crystal white towels folded into the shape of kissing swans. Our first-floor room opened to an outdoor common area and one of the nicest swimming pools we had ever seen. We explored our surroundings the day of our arrival but mostly settled in for bed, weary from spending the previous night on a bus.

The next morning, Nancy woke up to go for a run on the beach. In the midst of preparing, she noticed that Lily wasn't in her bed.

"Craig do you know where Lily is?" I heard Nancy say.

Remembering that there was a pool just a few steps from the front porch of our room, I was startled awake. I rubbed my eyes and looked toward the couch with ruffled sheets and blankets and even went to poke them to make sure Lily wasn't hidden underneath them.

"Lily?" I called out.

I checked the bathroom, which was empty, and continued calling out listening intently for some response. I hurriedly put on my clothes and rushed out to the pool to scan the water for a limp body floating facedown.

Almost every day as a parent there is a moment when you're not sure where your child is and in a mild state of alarm you call out their name. Almost always just as quickly as the alarms are sounded they are silenced as the child responds, "Here I am." So I ran around the pool, all the while calling out for Lily, expecting her to appear as she had every other time, only this time, there was no response. It was early and none of the other guests at the resort had emerged from their rooms yet. There was only silence and absence.

Nancy ran out to the beach as I continued scanning the pools. She came back to the room, winded from running. "Did you find her?"

"No!" I responded.

In disbelief, voice breaking, Nancy said, "What? Craig, where is she?!?!"

Before I had children I never understood the conventional wisdom that a parent's greatest fear is that their child will be abducted by a stranger. I thought it sounded so far-fetched, an example of parental paranoia, but then I had kids and it all made sense. It's highly unlikely but the possibility feels ever present, an everyday concern and reality:

Noel, did you brush your teeth?
Lily, did you finish your homework?

It's time to catch the bus for school.

Remember, don't talk to strangers at the bus stop.

It's the worst case scenario and it's constantly in the back of my mind. My daughter asks me if she can ride her bike alone to the end of the cul-de-sac and I hesitate to say yes because I fear that someone might swoop up next to her in a windowless van and take her away. So it's understandable that both Nancy and I quickly started to fear that Lily had been abducted. Our time at the orphanage in Chiang Rai loomed large in our imaginations as we ran to the front desk of the hotel to ask if they had seen her.

The seconds turned to minutes and we ran in opposite directions along the whole span of the beach. The thick sands made it feel like a nightmare where you're trying to run as fast as you can but instead you're stuck in slow motion, inescapable terror closing in. Two minutes passed that quickly became five minutes, and then ten minutes. We lost all social restraint and were yelling at the top of our lungs for help to find our daughter.

My heart pounded out of my chest as I ran all the way to the other side of the island scanning for any signs of Lily. Every person that crossed my path became a suspect in the abduction of my daughter. I walked uninvited through kitchens and living rooms of worker's homes that were embedded between the luxury hotels, wondering if she was being held in small corner closet. Memories of strangers who had remarked adoringly about Lily's beautiful pale skin went through my mind. I ran like every second counted, remembering that when a child is abducted the first minutes are the most important for successful recovery. When I reached the other beach I scanned the long boats bobbing in the shallow surf looking for signs of a boat sneaking away in the silence of the morning with a my daughter.

Nothing.

As I ran back hoping to see Nancy with Lily in tow, I thought about the vast mysterious country that we had experienced and about how infamous it was for exploiting young girls.

I made my way back to the hotel. Nancy and I saw each other, hoping to find assurance in the eyes of the other only to see new depths of despair.

Without anywhere else to look and with twenty minutes having passed with no response, we found ourselves in uncharted territory. Distant tragedies and injustices barged into our personal space like never before. The safety net that shielded us from the experience of the girls at the orphanage was shattered.

And then . . .

"We found her!" An employee of the hotel came running toward us.

"We found her. She's in the room," he repeated.

We ran back to the room and there she was. Nancy embraced her and everyone cried. For a good thirty minutes we all huddled together, and through jerky, oxygen-depriving tears, Lily explained that she got lost on the way back from an early morning trip to the beach.

We spent two more days at the resort, playing in the pool, swimming in the ocean, and enjoying beautiful sunsets, but it was hard to shake the trauma of touching so intimately the void of suffering and loss that Sirirat lives with every day at the orphanage.

Both girls got sick the night before we left, throwing up all over the room at the dormitory and all over the floor in front of the customs official at the airport. Our first purchase of the year was a brand new luxury tennis shirt from the duty free shop to replace Lily's barf-soaked T-shirt. It was her first piece of new clothing in twelve months, a Chris Evert signature edition.

CHAPTER 14

A Little Life

That is why faith, wherever it develops into hope, causes not rest but unrest, not patience but impatience. . . . Those who hope in Christ can no longer put up with reality as it is, but begin to suffer under it, to contradict it . . . for the goad of the promised future stabs inexorably into the flesh of every unfulfilled present.[1]
—Jürgen Moltmann

ONE STARTLING REALIZATION OF BEING THIRTY-NINE IS that when my parents were my age I was a senior in high school. I remember that around that time my dad read and recommended to me the book *Blue Highways*. I took him up on his offer and entered into William Least Heat-Moon's chronicle of three months traveling the back roads of America. Just thirty-eight years old and adrift in life, he christened his van "Ghost Dancer" and proceeded to discover his voice among two-calendar cafés and back-road strangers.

Toward the end of the book he observes, "I can't say, over the miles, that I had learned what I had wanted to know because I hadn't known what I wanted to know. But I did learn what I didn't know I wanted to know."[2]

When 2008 began, we didn't have a list of discoveries we expected to make. In the midst of feeling adrift in mindless consumption, we charted a course off the beaten path and have learned mostly what we didn't know we wanted to know—how to make butter, the ease of walking to school and work, the surprising sweetness of mashed rutabagas, how to make a flamingo piñata, the toll of an epic hail storm on a vegetable garden, how to cut up a whole chicken, how God's kingdom is often hiding in plain sight.

That book and quote have me wondering if this whole experiment has something to do with being thirty-nine years old. Maybe my thirty-nine-year-old dad handed me the book about a thirty-eight-year-old wanderer as if to say, "You'll be in your late thirties someday, too." All I have to say is if the most rebellious thing I do in midlife is take a Master Food Preserver class, I think I'm doing okay.

Gotta Have a Gimmick

"What's Wrong with Eco-Stunts?" That was the provocative lead for a 2009 *New Yorker* article about *No-Impact Man: The Adventures of a Guilty Liberal Who Attempts to Save the Planet, and the Discoveries He Makes about Himself and Our Way of Life in the Process*, the book and documentary movie that profile the year-long efforts of apartment-dwelling Manhattan urbanites to pull the plug on their environmental impact. But for Elizabeth Kolbert, the author of the article, the title wasn't a question, it was an explanatory statement, as in, "Let me tell you what's terribly wrong with eco-stunts." The article even had one of those famous *New Yorker* cartoons featuring a man sporting a Dudley Do-Right idealistic pose, wearing only leaves over his midsection, a triumphant candle in one hand and a switch to the power grid in the other. The subheading of the cartoon read, "The latest publishing fad features ecology as an extreme life style; the focus is on wacky misadventure, not global cataclysm." Needless to say, the article caught my attention. The cartoon character even looked a little bit like me.

We had insisted all along that we weren't setting out on some quest to save the world. We were mostly trying to save ourselves, gasping for fresh air in what seemed like a consumer wasteland. At various points along the way we entertained the idea of writing a book. A student at Washington State University was the first to broach the question.

She asked, "Why are you guys doing this? Are you going to write a book like Barbara Kingsolver?"

Without hesitating I said, "No. We see it as primarily a personal journey. We're glad to share what we're learning, but we have no plans other than sorting out more meaningful rhythms of consumption in the small space of our lives."

Obviously our answer to that question changed at some point. In fact it was just when we started to nail down the details of our own book with a publisher that the headline and cartoon from the *New Yorker* popped up on my computer screen.

The thesis of the article is that these high profile eco-stunts are a vaudevillian distraction from the real work of dealing with pressing environmental problems. The author acknowledges that there is a place for experiments on the margins of contemporary culture, lifting up Thoreau's *Walden* as a noble example. But Kolbert contends that where Walden begins with the words, "I went to the woods . . . to live deep and suck out all the marrow of life," these contemporary efforts should more accurately start with the line, "I went to the sustainability frontier to see if I could get a book deal." In the face of potential global cataclysm, the efforts of the Beavan family, or the Goodwin family for that matter, are nothing more than the "voluntary indulgence of a middle class family."[3]

Ms. Kolbert goes on to suggest a more worthy book project for Mr. Beavan. Instead of turning off the power to his single apartment he should spend a year organizing the other residents of the building to install more efficient heating systems. Instead of living for a year without toilet paper, he should go to the state capital and lobby lawmakers to institute more earth friendly waste management systems. Instead of riding bikes and scooters around Manhattan, the family should go to Washington D.C. and demand that Congress pass climate-change legislation. With a flurry of fine-tuned New York worthy sarcasm, the article concludes, "Here's a possible title for the book: *Impact Man*."[4]

On behalf of the Beavan family and anyone else who has ever written a personal account of their efforts to live a more just and sustainable life, I'd like say, "Ouch! That hurts."

The article continues to raise some important questions for me as I contemplate the sum of our journey. Even more than criticizing a trend in publishing, the article touches on an important fault line in current debates about sustainability and going green. As more and more people seek responsibility in their consumer lives—forgoing plastic bags at the grocery store, buying local food at the farmers' market, and replacing light bulbs—many are quick to dismiss such efforts, pointing to the cruel mathematics of global carbon and consumption statistics. The argument is that the only way to make a difference is in the political realm of regulation and legislation. It's nice and quaint to turn your lawn into a vegetable garden and can your own pickles, but such actions are almost entirely meaningless in the face of a global environmental crisis.

A Little Life

Ultimately I don't have a defense to offer when it comes to questions about the worth of our efforts. Our actions, for the most part, were arbitrary, illogical, and ultimately indefensible. But in many ways, that was the whole point, to do things that don't compute, to intentionally follow labyrinthine pathways in a world stuck in ruts of commodified efficiency, to choose relationships over saving twenty cents a pound on ground beef, to waste time with the kids, to stock up on pineapple and tuna fish from Thailand and at the same time refuse to buy cottage cheese from Seattle, to push our children like a pack of mules on Halloween night in order to stock up on chocolate and caramel, to walk home from work at the end of the day in the middle of winter, to exercise our rebellion against consumerism by spending twenty bucks on a tin of cheese, and as if that isn't enough nonsense, to envision it all as a spiritual discipline, a meeting place of God's unfolding kingdom and our attempts at faithfulness.

While I don't have a defense to offer, I couldn't disagree more with the premise that our actions don't somehow matter in the whole scope of things. Far from setting things straight, the vision of outsourcing meaningful responsibility to governments, agencies, and organizations reflects a particular sickness of the modern world.

In his essay, "Think Little," Wendell Berry explains:

> We need better government, no doubt about it. But we also . . . need persons and households that do not have to wait upon organizations, but can make necessary changes in themselves, on their own. . . . A man (or woman) who is willing to undertake the discipline and the difficulty of mending his (or her) own ways is worth more to the conservation movement than a hundred who are insisting merely that the government and the industries mend their ways. If you are concerned about the proliferation of trash, then by all means start an organization in your community to do something about it. But before—and while—you organize, pick up some cans and bottles yourself. . . . If you talk a good line without being changed by what you say, then you are not just hypocritical and doomed; you have become an agent of the disease.[5]

Our year taught us the power of thinking little. Simple, small choices were the gateway to the large complex issues we faced. It was only when we started farming our own backyard that our eyes were opened to the farming practices in the wheat fields of our region. It wasn't until we saw our own chickens bathing in the afternoon sun that we came to understand the horror of confinement-cage methods used by large egg producers. The small act of paying attention to the labels on food at the grocery store woke us up to the plight of local farmers. Ironically, thinking little also recently led me to testify before state senators in Olympia, advocating for a new law protecting the property tax exemption of nonprofits throughout the state who host farmers' markets. Without walking in the little details of our community I would have had no idea how to speak to the big picture at the capital building.

An Act of Hope

Looking back on the journey I can see how our faith played a particularly important role in our commitment to thinking little.

In the opening chapter of this book I quoted Wendell Berry's famous line, "Eating is an agricultural act." I want to expand on that and say overtly what I have been suggesting throughout the book: eating is a theological act, with deep connections not only to land but to the Creator of the land. More than that, buying food or anything else, is a theological act. For those of us who claim an ultimate allegiance to the Jesus who is redeeming all things (Col. 1:20), decisions about what we purchase or don't purchase are vital expressions of our faith. In a world where everything is being gathered up "in Christ" (Eph. 1:10) we are invited to join in, seeking justice and peace by what we gather up in our arms at the shopping mall and grocery store. The Christian church brings a unique orientation of faith and hopefulness to these issues of environment and consumption. In my opinion, this faith in the God who is saving the world is the church's greatest gift to an environmental movement that struggles to make sense of small actions in the face of global crises.

In the spring of 2008, just as we were getting our bearings, I read an article by Michael Pollan in the *New York Times* magazine that serves as an interesting contrast to the cynical *New Yorker* article. Under the title "Why Bother?" Pollan describes the complex dilemma facing individuals making choices in a global village:

> Is eating local or walking to work really going to reduce my carbon footprint? According to one analysis, if walking to work increases your appetite and you consume more meat or milk as a result, walking might actually emit more carbon than driving. A handful of studies have recently suggested that in certain cases under certain conditions, produce from places as far away as New Zealand might account for less carbon than comparable domestic products. True, at least one of these studies was co-written by a representative of agribusiness interests in (surprise!) New Zealand, but even so, they make you wonder. If determining the carbon footprint of food is really this complicated, and I've got to consider not only "food miles: but also whether the food came by ship or truck and how lushly the grass grows in New Zealand, then maybe on second thought I'll just buy the imported chops at Costco, at least until the experts get their footprints sorted out.[6]

Pollan's article came out in the midst of our year. So there we were, faithfully feeding our children weeds from the garden and tearing out the lawn, when we got this heavy-duty question dropped in our laps. What if the Goodwin-family experiment didn't amount to anything in the end? What if at the end of the year we were left to say, "I went a year without sugar, and all I got was this T-shirt from Thailand?" Our daily activities were never too many steps removed from this bothersome question.

But at the end of his article, Pollan suggests an orientation of hope that both transcends the circumstances on the ground and more deeply anchors us in those very circumstances saying, "Going personally green is a bet, nothing more or less, though it's one we probably all should make, even if the odds of it paying off aren't great. Sometimes you have to act as if acting will make a difference, even when you can't prove that it will."[7]

He is saying that it takes faith, and I couldn't agree more. This is where the church has a particularly important perspective to share. The gift of faith in Jesus is not just that it secures us a place in heaven, but that it also secures us a place of hopeful action in the world. I like the way the preacher from the book of Hebrews puts it: "Now faith is being sure of what we hope for and certain of what we do not see" (11:1). It's a tenacious orientation of hopefulness in the midst of the everyday. It's a conviction that the primary plotline I find myself a part of is redemption and that my daily actions are somehow part of that grand story.

That's why I bother.

About five months into our year we arrived at a strange and surprising place as we gathered for dinner. I was comfortably snug in my second-hand shoes and sweaty from the bike ride home from work. Nancy was fashionably attired in her thrift store dress. The girls were fresh from a joyful jaunt in the garden maze, and we were all eager to dig into some local asparagus, field greens, homemade bread, home-churned butter, and meatloaf made from deer meat provided by a hunting friend. About halfway through the meal, it dawned on me that I hadn't given any of these things a second thought. All of these practices were normal. We'd gone from wondering if it was even possible to follow these rules, to having them be a new, no-big-deal normal.

Our previous patterns of consumption had seemed so unchangeable. It was just the way the world was (or so we thought), and it was hard to imagine that there were other options. But we were learning that all habits, patterns, and practices of consumption are changeable. It might take five or six months to feel comfortable with them, but nothing was inevitable or set in stone. All it took was an intentional focus on the little things and some faith that not only could we do it but that somehow it mattered if we did.

So these are the lessons we were learning. Think little and have faith. Plant a garden, set up a chicken coop in the laundry room, eat weeds, spend more on visits to the farmers' market than on visits to the doctor, walk slowly, ask questions, make friends, consider the lilies and let the big picture emerge one small adventure at a time.

EPILOGUE

The adventure continues to unfold for the Goodwin family in 2010. As I write we're basking in the glow of having just secured the coveted grand champion largest onion at the Spokane County fair. The labyrinth garden is wrapping up its third growing season and I even found a way to expand my gardening footprint by helping start a community garden down the road from the church. The Millwood Paper Mill has made up to six acres of land available for community gardening so there is plenty of room to expand in future years.

One recent afternoon Nancy and I came home and were approached by a teenage neighbor who asked, "Are you the people with the chickens?" Our five hens had apparently escaped and wandered into someone's driveway two blocks away. I got my chicken shepherd stick and corralled them back home along a busy street. It was officially the first chicken stampede in our neighborhood. I still refuse to eat industrial chicken, and given the recent recall of eggs, we're more glad than ever to have a safe supply from our happy hens. We've added Nibbles the rabbit to our small farm and look forward to showing him at the fair next year.

We continue to get a large portion of our food from local farmers and continue to nurture those connections.

Not long after getting back from Thailand we bought a used minivan and returned to a two-car life. But we still walk the kids to school and I ride my bike to work when I can.

Nancy still stocks us with fresh loaves of bread every week, and we've taken to grinding our own flour. But I haven't made butter in a while and the ice-cream maker doesn't get near the use it used to.

We continue to improvise our consumer lives in the midst of all the complexities and compromises that come with deciding what to buy or not to buy. And we look back on our year of plenty with an abundance of gratitude.

In her book *Bird by Bird: Some Instructions on Writing and Life*, Anne Lamott tells writers that one of the keys to writing is short assignments and small picture frames. Instead of setting out on some grand scheme to write the next *Brothers Karamazov*, the thing to do is pick one small assignment, one picture that fits into a small, one-inch frame, and go to work writing about it, describing it, fleshing it out. She quotes E. L. Doctorow who said, "Writing a novel is like driving a car at night. You can see only as far as your headlights but you can make the whole trip that way." I agree with Lamott when she says, "This is right up there with the best advice about writing, or life."[8] Our journey was in many ways an exercise in paying attention, one small picture frame at a time.

Notes

CHAPTER 1

1. www.noimpactman.typepad.com (accessed 8/15/10).

2. Michael Pollan, *The Omnivore's Dilemma: A Natural History of Four Meals* (New York: Penguin, 2006), 11.

3. Richard B. Gregg, *The Value of Voluntary Simplicity* (Wallingford, Penn.: Pendle Hill, 1936).

4. Duane Elgin, *Voluntary Simplicity: Toward a Way of Life that is Outwardly Simply, Inwardly Rich*, 2nd rev. ed. (New York: Harper Collins, 2010), xxvi.

5. Annie Leonard, *The Story of Stuff*, (New York: Free Press, 2010), 158.

6. Wendell Berry, "Health is Membership" (speech delivered at a spirituality and healing conference, Louisville, Kentucky, October 17, 1994).

7. Doris Janzen Longacre, *More-with-Less Cookbook* (Scottdale, Penn.: Herald Press, 1976), 12.

8. www.nutritionj.com (accessed 9/21/10).

9. www.globalrichlist.com (accessed 9/21/10).

SECTION I

1. Parker Palmer, *Let Your Life Speak* (San Francisco: John Wiley & Sons, 2000) 99–100.

2. I owe this phrase to Joseph Sittler's *The Care of the Earth, and Other University Sermons* (Minneapolis: Fortress Press, 1964), 28.

3. Judith Shulevitz, *The Sabbath World: Glimpses of a Different Order of Time* (New York: Random House, 2010), 5.

CHAPTER 2

1. Mirslov Volf, *Against the Tide: Love in a Time of Petty Dreams and Persisting Enmities* (Grand Rapids, Mich.: Wm. B. Eerdmans, 2010), 141.

2. Clemens Sedmak, *Doing Local Theology: A Guide for Artisans of a New Humanity* (Maryknoll, N.Y.: Orbis Books, 2002), 2.

3. Elizabeth Henderson, *Sharing the Harvest: A Citizen's Guide to Community Supported Agriculture.* (White River Junction, Vt.: Chelsea Green Publishing Company, 1999), xvi.

CHAPTER 3

1. Wendell Berry, *The Art of the Commonplace: The Agrarian Essays of Wendell Berry,* ed. Norman Wirzba (Berkeley: Counterpoint, 2002), 154.

2. Rev. Boniface Verheyen, trans., *The Holy Rule of St. Benedict, The 1949 Edition,* www.holyrule.com (accessed 9/21/10).

3. D. Stephen Long, *Divine Economy: Theology and the Market* (New York: Routledge, 2000).

4. Ibid., 265.

CHAPTER 4

1. www.freehugscampaign.org (accessed 9/21/10).

2. http://www.campuscrusade.com/fourlawseng.htm

3. Lesslie Newbigin, *The Gospel in a Pluralist Society* (Grand Rapids, Mich.: Wm. B. Eerdmans, 1989), 15.

4. Alasdair McIntyre, *After Virtue: A Study in Moral Theory* (London: Gerald Duckworth & Co., 1984), 216.

5. Rodney Clapp, *The Consuming Passion: Christianity & the Consumer Culture* (Downers Grove, Il.: InterVarsity Press, 1998), 12.

Section II

1. Wendell Berry, *The Art of the Commonplace*, 24.

Chapter 5

1. Wendell Berry, "The Idea of a Local Economy," *Orion*, winter 2001, www.orionmagazine.org (accessed August 12, 2010).

2. David R. Montgomery, *Dirt: The Erosion of Civilizations* (Berkely: University of California Press, 2007), 19.

3. Ibid., 4.

4. Ibid., 209.

Chapter 6

1. Morris Allen Grubbs, ed., *Conversations with Wendell Berry*, (Jackson: University Press of Mississippi, 2007), 75.

2. Eugene Peterson, *The Wisdom of Each Other: A Conversation between Spiritual Friends* (Grand Rapids, Mich.: Zondervan, 1998), 80.

3. Denise Roy, *My Monastery Is a Minivan: Where the Daily Is Divine and the Routine Becomes Prayer* (Chicago: Loyola Press, 2001), 15.

Chapter 7

1. Wendell Berry, "The Country of Marriage," in *The Collected Poems of Wendell Berry, 1957–1982* (New York: North Point Press, 1987).

2. Eugene Peterson, *Under the Upredictable Plant: An Exploration in Vocational Holiness* (Grand Rapids, Mich.: Eerdmans, 1992), 75.

3. www.theholidayspot.com (accessed 9/21/10).

4. Victor Lebow, "Price Competition in 1955," *The Journal of Retailing*: (spring 1955), 7.

5. Travis J. Carter and Thomas Gilovich, "The Relative Relativity of Material and Experiential Purchases," *Journal of Personality and Social Psychology* (January 2010).

6. Peterson, *Under the Unpredictable Plant*, 89.

7. Interview at Atlantic Online, "*The Atlantic*: American Ideas: How Has HIV Changed Your Life?" www.clicker.com/web/the-atlantic-american-ideas/How-Has-HIV-Changed-Your-Life-540807/ (accessed 9/21/10).

8. Peterson, *Under the Unpredictable Plant*, 90.

CHAPTER 8

1. Alfred Austin, *The Garden That I Love*. (London: Adam and Charles Black, 1906), 98.

2. Ibid., 11.

3. Cedarfield Plantation Homeowner's Asssociation Rules, www.cedarfieldplantation.com (accessed 9/21/10).

4. H. C. Flores, *Food Not Lawns* (White River Junction, Vt.: Chelsea Green Publishing, 2006), 12.

5. Matthew B. Crawford, *Shopclass as Soulcraft: An Inquiry Into the Value of Work* (New York: Penguin Press, 2009), 59, 60.

6. Wendell Berry, *A Continuous Harmony: Essays Cultural and Agricultural* (Washington, D.C.: Shoemaker & Hoard, 1971, 1972), 80, 81.

7. Ibid., 81.

CHAPTER 9

1. Wendell Berry, *A Continuous Harmony: Essays Cultural and Agricultural* (Washington, D.C.: Shoemaker & Hoard, 1971, 1972), 4, 5.

2. Elizabeth Gilbert, *Eat, Pray, Love* (New York: Penguin Group, 2006), 12.

3. Wendell Berry, *Standing by Words* (Washington, D.C.: Shoemaker & Hoard, 1983), 70.

4. Darrel L. Guder, ed., *Missional Church: A Vision for the Sending of the Church in North America* (Grand Rapids, Mich.: Eerdmans, 1998), 93–94.

5. Zygmunt Bauman, *Liquid Modernity* (Malden, Mass.: Blackwell, 2000), 201.

6. Alan Roxburgh introduced me to the concept of leaders as poetic miners in the Missional Leadership cohort at Fuller Seminary. See his book *The Missionary Congregation, Leadership, and Liminality* for further exploration of this theme.

7. Russell Shorto, *Descartes' Bones: A Skeletal History of the Conflict Between Faith and Reason* (New York: Vintage Books, 2008), 62.

8. Ibid., 179–180.

9. Richard J. Mouw, *The Smell of Sawdust* (Grand Rapids, Mich.: Zondervan, 2000), 145.

Chapter 10

1. Wendell Berry, *The Art of the Commonplace: The Agrarian Essays of Wendall Berry*, ed. Norman Wirzba (Berkeley: Counterpoint, 2002), 326.

2. Rich Mouw, *On Letting Chickens Strut Their Stuff*, www.beliefnet.com (accessed 9/22/10).

3. American Meat Institute, www.meatami.com (accessed 9/21/10).

4. Peter Lennox, "Pecking Order," *Times Higher Education*: (February 4, 2010), www.timeshighereducation.co.uk (accessed 9/21/10).

Section IV

1. Donald Culross Peattie, *An Almanac for Moderns*. (New York: G.P. Putnam's Sons, 1935), 394.

Chapter 11

1. http://blog.algore.com/2010/01/green_pastors

2. David Kinnaman, *Unchristian: What a New Generation Really Thinks about Christianity . . . and Why It Matters* (Grand Rapids, Mich.: Baker Books, 2007), 46.

3. Ibid., 46.

4. Ibid., 46–47.

5. www.religions.pewforum.org (accessed 9/21/10).

6. Linnie Marsh Wolfe, *Son of the Wilderness: The Life of John Muir.* (Madison: University of Wisconsin Press, 2003), 179.

CHAPTER 13

1. Ntozake Shange, *Nappy Edges* (New York: St. Martin's Press, 1972), 114–16.

2. From church newsletter, International Church of Bangkok, February 2009, www.icbangkok.org (accessed 9/21/10).

CHAPTER 14

1. Jürgen Moltmann, *Theology of Hope* (Minneapolis: Fortress Press, 1993), 21.

2. William Least Heat-Moon, *Blue Highways* (New York: Little, Brown and Co., 1982), 411.

3. Elizabeth Kolbert, "Green Like Me," *The New Yorker.* (August 31, 2009), www.newyorker.com (accessed 9/22/10).

4. Ibid.

5. Wendell Berry, *A Continuous Harmony: Essays Cultural and Agricultural* (Washington, D.C.: Shoemaker & Hoard, 1971, 1972), 78–79.

6. Michael Pollan, "Why Bother," *The New York Times*, April 20, 2008, nytimes.com (accessed 8/15/10).

7. Ibid.

8. Anne Lamott, *Bird by Bird: Some Instructions on Writing and Life* (New York: Anchor Books, 1994), 18.

APPENDIX A

A Brief Explanation of My Obsession with Wendell Berry

I WAS FIRST INTRODUCED TO THE WRITING OF WENDELL BERRY BY Eugene Peterson. More than ten years ago I was at a pastor's conference where Peterson was speaking. He had included Berry's book, *What Are People For?*, on his list of recommended reading. I found myself wondering why he thought an agrarian poet/farmer was an important voice for a group of pastors to listen to. (Peterson has famously said of Berry's influence, that when he comes across the word farm in Berry's written works, he replaces it in his mind with the word congregation.)

I bought a copy of *What Are People For?* at the conference but it sat unread and gathering dust on my bookshelf for years. Early on in our year of plenty, that book came off the shelf and Berry's words found fertile ground in my mind and heart. As I read through his essays, he became my second John Muir, the pioneer who had been to beautiful, wide-open spaces and described his adventures with such eloquence and passion that I, too, wanted to go. In many ways, Berry was a tour guide for our family as we navigated through the issues of food, land, farming, and faith. In the development of this manuscript, it seemed natural that he would play a similar role for the readers of this book.

Like Peterson, Berry is now on my list of writers and thinkers that pastors and churches need to hear from in these fragmented times. I hope the many references to his work here will encourage a new group of people to take his books off the shelf and give them a proper reading.

APPENDIX B

Plant With Purpose

Plant With Purpose is a Christian humanitarian organization headquartered in San Diego that is dedicated to helping the rural poor. They have a presence in Haiti, Latin America, Africa, and Thailand, among other places. They are unique in that they approach Christian concerns about poverty and injustice through the lenses of reforestation and environmental sustainability.

This is how they describe their story on their Web site, www.plantwithpurpose.org: For us, the breakthrough came when we saw firsthand the connection between poverty and the environment. Many people think of poverty and the environment as separate issues, but in fact they are hugely interdependent. Most of the world's poor are rural poor. Many are subsistence farmers, completely dependent on their environment for survival. But as a result of widespread deforestation, the land isn't providing like it used to.

Land that once bore bountiful crops that could be sold or eaten, isn't producing. Streams that used to provide water to drink, now run dry. Out of desperation, the poor cut down more trees to sell as firewood, even though doing so means further destroying their one chance of survival.

By reversing deforestation, Plant With Purpose helps the poor restore productivity to their land to create economic opportunity out of environmental restoration. Since 1984 we have helped more than 100,000 people in some 230 villages lift themselves out of poverty through our holistic approach to sustainable development.

The church I pastor partners with Plant With Purpose at Christmas and Easter. Instead of buying a small forest of poinsettias and Easter lilies, which in the past were often wasted, we now invite the congregation to take the money they would have spent on those plants and make a donation to Plant With Purpose. The $15 that would have purchased a temporary glimmer of Christmas cheer or Easter joy goes to plant fifteen trees in deforested regions around the world.

Here's how we explain it to the congregation:

Christmas is the celebration of the new life we have in Christ, a life that grows and is sustained over time. While poinsettias are one symbol of new life, another fitting metaphor is the tree. Isaiah uses this image of God's redeeming work in Isaiah 41:19-20,

> I will put in the desert the cedar and the acacia, the myrtle and the olive. I will set pines in the wasteland, the fir and the cypress together, so that people may see and know, may consider and understand, that the hand of the LORD has done this, and the Holy One of Israel has created it.

Isaiah's cedars and acacias can appropriately be called, Christmas Trees. After a long-standing tradition of ordering poinsettias for our Christmas Eve services, we invite the congregation to embrace the trees planted by Plant With Purpose as Christmas trees that will stand as enduring witnesses to the reconciling work of God in the world.

Plant With Purpose is a wonderful resource for churches that want to get involved in creation care but are not sure how that fits with traditional conceptions of mission. The organization both helps interpret the convergence of environmental concern and Christian faith, and invites people into meaningful action and participation.

Scott Sabin, the Director of Plant With Purpose, has written an excellent book, *Tending to Eden: Environmental Stewardship for God's People*, that describes in detail the work of this fine organization.

APPENDIX C

How to Turn Your Lawn into a Vegetable Garden and Other Random Gardening Advice

BEFORE YOU TEAR OUT THE LAWN YOU'LL WANT TO DO A survey of your physical space and identify every area of your property that gets at least six hours of direct sunlight. Vegetable plants are nature's version of solar panels. They harvest the sun's energy and package it in tasty morsels of consumable energy. A good exercise would be to think about where you would put solar panels on your property. That will give you the right instincts for thinking about where to grow vegetables—south facing and maximum direct sunlight. It might be helpful to draw a rough map of your property and identify the spaces that meet the above requirements.

When you do the survey you'll probably discover you've already got stuff growing in those places and most of that stuff is probably grass. There are two ways to replace a lawn with vegetable garden plots:

1) Raised Beds: You can use raised beds constructed of two-by-eight douglas-fir lumber. Don't use treated wood. You'll likely get a good dose of arsenic and other nasty chemical with any vegetables you grow in a treated-wood raised bed. The ideal garden bed is about four feet wide by eight-to-ten feet long. You can assemble beds using 2.5 inch outdoor wood screws to connect the corners or

use a four-by-four on the inside of each corner and secure the two-by-eights with nails or screws in the four-by-four.

Build the beds, and place them directly over the lawn with landscape cloth covering the bottom of the bed where the grass is growing. Fill the bed with gardening soil and start gardening. At the end of the first growing season, use a pitchfork to loosen the soil and poke lots of holes in the fabric, which will make openings for future plant roots to go deep into the soil—don't do that the first year or grass will grow up through the fabric. The book, *All New Square Foot Gardening*, by Mel Bartholomew is a helpful resource for making the most of this kind of gardening.

2) Removing Sod and Creating Rows: The other strategy is to use a sod cutter to remove the grass. After removing the sod and stacking it somewhere to be used as compost for later, add composted manure to the soil and mix it together using a rototiller.

I recommend using a no-till method of gardening (after getting your garden bed finished) with designated gardening rows with permanent pathways. The theory is that you never step on the garden beds and stay on the path. The path gets packed down and the soil beds don't which means you won't have to rototill every year. That's not just a nice break for you, it's actually better for the garden. The mechanical vibrations from regular rototilling create a hardpan under the top six inches of tilled soil, which means roots can't grow very deep, which in turn leads to a reduced yield. *The Vegetable Gardener's Bible* by Ed Smith is a good resource for understanding this method of gardening.

My friends and neighbors Bob and Bonnie Gregson, authors of the book, *Rebirth of the Small Family Farm*, helped complete my education on the art of no-till gardening. They recommend the technique of using a pitchfork. Here's how it works: to prepare your garden beds for a new season, cover them with compost, then poke the soil repeatedly with the pitchfork moving it gently back and forth with each penetration of the soil. This helps in a couple of ways: the new compost falls into the holes, helping the compost get into the soil, and it aerates the soil. It does all of this without destroying the delicate ecosystem of worms and worm holes. The worms have been working all winter and it's a shame to ruin all their hard work.

If you choose this method of gardening, I recommend covering the pathways with layers of nonglossy newspaper, covered by a generous layer of straw. This will limit the battle against weeds to the actual garden beds. Over time, the newspaper and straw will compost into the soil. Be careful not to use hay, which is full of seeds. Bark and pine straw are also not recommended because they take longer to compost.

Planting Your Garden

Pay attention to the seed spacing advice on the seed packet. This is my Achilles' heel of gardening. I almost always crowd the plants. Sometimes this works in my favor. For example, peppers like to be crowded. They like to be tucked together to keep the humidity up and provide some protection from intense heat. Carrots on the other hand will simply not grow much if you don't give them adequate room. This goes for all root crops. Take note that the seed pack will indicate the recommended spacing when planting as well as the recommended spacing after the plants start growing—you do this by thinning small sprouts. If you use all the seeds, keep the seed pack around to double check the thinning requirements. One caveat to all of this is that the seed packs make their recommendations based on traditional row crops.

If you're working with a small space, there are alternative methods of spacing that will maximize plants. Instead of planting your corn in a row, plant it in a small circle. Instead of planting your carrots in a row, scatter them in a bunch and thin out as required. If you have limited space, consider going vertical. Instead of planting bush beans, plant pole beans. You also might want to consider getting a bush variety of some plants instead of creeping plants that hog space. Cucumbers and pumpkins/squash, which are notorious for taking over the garden, all come in space-saving "bush" varieties.

Another key to successful gardening, year after year, is rotating crops to limit disease. For example tomato, potato, and eggplant varieties should not be planted in the same place from one year to the next. Rotation is also important for not depleting the soil. You want to follow heavy to medium feeders that draw a lot of nutrients from the soil (tomatoes, corn, cabbage, peppers) with either light feeders (carrots, beets, onions) or heavy givers (beans, peas) that actually fix nitrogen in the soil and enrich it. I like the methodology that recommends a rotation of heavy feeders followed with heavy givers which are then followed by light feeders.

If you lack space or sunshine to grow plants on your own property, I encourage you to look for a nearby community garden that rents out garden plots for the summer. If you don't find any, consider starting one! There are a growing number of networks like Urban Garden Share (www.urbangardenshare.org) in Seattle, that will match landless gardeners with homeowners who are willing to make their yards available for gardeners, usually in return for a share of the harvest.

Appendix D

How to Raise Chickens
in Your Backyard

BEFORE YOU BRING HOME A BOX FULL OF CHIRPING chicks, make sure to check with your local zoning ordinances and neighborhood association rules to see if chickens are allowed in your vicinity. Most ordinances for residential neighborhoods allow three to five chickens and have provisions regarding the proximity of the coop to buildings and property lines. Many cities have not caught up with this growing trend and do not have ordinances in place. If you're interested in getting involved in changing the laws, the Chicken Revolution (www.salemchickens.com) offers a front-row seat to one example of how the law was changed in one American city.

BUILDING A CHICKEN COOP

When I went about the task of designing our coop, I found some great resources like www.backyardchickens.com that had an abundance of ideas about how to put a coop together. The problem for me is that I didn't have a lot of experience with construction, and I couldn't find step-by-step instructions for a design that met our needs. I checked out several books from the library that had chicken coop designs, but again, none of them quite fit the bill. For a while we scanned Craigslist for used chicken coops, but thought better of it because of concerns about transferring disease to the new chicks. In the end we created our own design and despite a lack of construction experience managed to put it together, and two years later it's still standing.

The key rule of thumb for designing a coop is that there should be four square feet per bird in the enclosed coop part and ten square feet per bird for the run. The run is a caged area where the chickens have room to strut their stuff. I highly recommend a dirt/sand floor for the run, with a roof of some kind covering it. The only time odor can be a problem is when the run gets wet. Our covered run keeps the floor dry and the chicken poop turns to dust and is filtered into the dirt.

Based on our experience, chickens like to range free beyond the run. Your hens will be much happier if you create a way for them to roam beyond their allotted ten square feet. When we're home, we open the door to the run and allow them to roam the yard, bathe in the sun, eat worms, take dust baths, and, in general, wander as they please. It's easy to clip their wings to keep them from escaping a fenced area. A pair of muck boots come in handy for trips to the coop. Detailed pictures of our award-winning coop design are available at www.yearofplenty.org.

SELECTING AND PURCHASING YOUR CHICKENS:

We've really enjoyed having a variety of chickens, as opposed to picking just one breed. McMurray's (www.mcmurrayhatchery.com) is a good place to start in learning about different breeds of chickens. It is a hatchery that will mail you chickens if you are ordering twenty-five or more, but their site is also full of great information. Most farm supply stores and pet stores have chicks available for purchase, especially in the springtime.

We've had great luck with one Buff Orpington, two Silver Laced Wyandottes, a Golden Laced Wyandotte, and an Ameracauna that lays green eggs. Our girls picked them out so our selection process wasn't too scientific.

Gary Angell from Rocky Ridge Ranch near Spokane has a wealth of information on breeds. Gary's favorite bird for the home garden is the Buff Orpington. It's a large, hardy bird, it will continue laying through the winter, and it's gentle with a good disposition for kids. Based on our experience, I agree. My one caveat is that the large comb of the Orpington can have issues with frostbite unless you heat the coop or insulate and fully enclose it. Breeds with a tighter comb may be a better choice for very cold climates.

Gary's next recommendation is the Australorp because it's a big bird that matures faster than others and has larger eggs than most. The other breeds he speaks highly of are the Barred Rock and the New Hampshire Red. The Wyandottes are generally smaller birds and produce smaller eggs, but they are beautiful and have a good disposition, although they are more flighty than the Buff Orpington. The Ameracaunas are also smaller with smaller eggs, but the beautiful green hue of their eggs makes them a worthwhile addition to a backyard flock.

Other tidbits of wisdom from Gary:

Don't buy Sex-Links, which are crossbred to make identifying their sex at birth easier.

Rhode Island Reds are "ornery" and will peck and bully other breeds of birds.

Make sure the birds are sexed, meaning that they have been identified as hens or roosters, otherwise you're likely to get half roosters and half hens. Take note that it's not necessary to have a rooster to have eggs. You only need a rooster if you want the eggs to hatch chicks.

There is a big problem with Merrick's disease, and Gary advises requesting that the birds get vaccinated when they are one day old. This may be less of a problem with backyard farmers.

If you want to raise a turkey, put the little turkey in with the chicks, and it will actually be good for the turkey. The chicks are smarter than the turkey and will help the turkey navigate the early days. You can separate them later.

Most of these breeds have been bred for eggs and make scrawny meat birds even if they say they are described as good for meat.

The Cornish variety are the only kinds of real meat birds available to people in the United States. They have the large breast and legs that we're used to eating. Gary says they are brain-dead birds who are bred to be raised in large meat bird operations. They won't do much free ranging even if given the opportunity. He laments that, unlike other countries, we don't have other varieties of meat birds available.

APPENDIX E

The Basics of Home Food Preservation

FOOD PRESERVATION CAN BE A WONDERFUL ADDITION TO A HOUSE-hold's seasonal rhythms of eating. If you are going to take up can-ning fruits and vegetables, there are a few key myths regarding safety that are important to note (remember, I'm a Master Food Preserver):

Just because the jars are sealed does not mean the food is safe. The heat penetration into the jars makes the food safe by killing all the bacteria; the seal keeps it safe. If the food isn't safe in the first place, the seal doesn't matter. There are a few sealing methods that might get a seal but don't kill bacteria—using an iron on top of the can, using the oven to heat them up, and running them through the dishwasher (yes, someone actually did that). Basically, any method other than the one specified in the recipe from a science-based source is unsafe. For the proven recipes, scientists actually put probes into the cans with the particular recipe to take the tem-perature throughout the can, and determine how long it takes for the heat to penetrate. Different foods conduct heat at different rates, so no guessing is allowed.

Just because you've used the same recipe and method for many years without problems does not mean it's safe. In my Master Food Preserver class, we heard the story of a couple who used the same unsafe recipe for fifty years without a problem, but in year fifty-one, it was a killer.

Just because the food looks fine doesn't mean it's okay to eat.

Just because your friend who gives you homemade pickles is too nice to try to kill you, doesn't mean that they won't inadvertently put you in danger with their family recipe from the 1800s. If you receive canned foods as a gift, it's always good to inquire about the recipe that was used. If you give canned foods as a gift, the friendly thing to do is attach the recipe and offer assurances that you used a scientifically tested recipe.

The big lesson regarding safety and food preservation is that you have to follow scientifically tested canning recipes. Save the culinary flourishes for when you serve the food. The good news is that if you follow proven recipes faithfully, the food will be safe to eat. The National Center for Home Food Preservation (www.uga.edu/nchfp/) and the *Ball Complete Book of Home Preserving* are reliable sources backed up by good science. The NCHFP also has a book and DVD version of the recipes called *So Easy to Preserve*. I hate to say it, but old canning cookbooks are not a good source of recipes because of changes that have been made in the guidelines due to new research.

OTHER RANDOM TIPS FOR HOME PRESERVATION:

Make sure to adjust water-bath time for altitude.

Steam canners have major problems and are not recommended as a replacement for water-bath canning.

Vacuum-packing machines are not a substitute for heat processing home-canned foods.

Use jars made for canning and lids with screw bands.

Using metal scrubbers to clean jars can weaken them and lead to breakage.

Screwing the band on too tight can lead to the lid buckling.

Check your appliance manufacturer's recommendations before you can on a ceramic stovetop.

It is not considered safe to can quick breads.

It is also not safe to home preserve vegetables in oil, so throw out that garlic in oil your cousin gave you and that oil that you added peppers to last summer for the fun of it. The oil creates an anaerobic environment that can lead to the growth of botulism toxin. Some things we see in the store can't be safely prepared in the home.

The companion Web site to this book, www.yearofplenty.org, has a wealth of other information on home food preservation.